A GUIDED TOUR THROUGH HISTORY

The Freedom Trail: Boston

HELP US KEEP THIS GUIDE UP TO DATE

We would love to hear from you concerning your experiences with this guide and how you feel it could be improved and kept up to date. Please send your comments and suggestions to:

editorial@GlobePequot.com

Thanks for your input, and happy travels!

A Timeline Book

A GUIDED TOUR THROUGH HISTORY

The Freedom Trail: Boston

ANNA MANTZARIS

Photographs by Saroyan Humphrey

travel

Guilford, Connecticut

An imprint of Globe Pequot Press

Library of Congress Cataloging-in-Publication Data is available on file.

ISBN 978-0-7627-5741-1

Printed in China
10 9 8 7 6 5 4 3 2 1

All the information in this guidebook is subject to change. We recommend that you call ahead to obtain current information before traveling. All restaurants are open daily for breakfast, lunch, and dinner, unless otherwise noted.

Contents

Introduction 1
Key Participants 8
Tour Stop 1: Boston Common 12
Tour Stop 2: Massachusetts State House 17
Tour Stop 3: Park Street Church 21
Tour Stop 4: Granary Burying Ground 24
Tour Stop 5: King's Chapel 26
Tour Stop 6: First Public School/Statue of Benjamin Franklin 29
Tour Stop 7: Old Corner Bookstore 33
Tour Stop 8: Old South Meeting House 35
Tour Stop 9: Old State House Museum 40
Tour Stop 10: Boston Massacre Site 44
Tour Stop 11: Faneuil Hall 47
Tour Stop 12: Paul Revere House 51
Tour Stop 13: Old North Church 57
Tour Stop 14: Copp's Hill Burying Ground 62
Tour Stop 15: USS *Constitution* ("Old Ironsides") 64
Tour Stop 16: Bunker Hill Monument 69
Boston: A Tourist's Guide to Exploring, Staying, and Eating 73
Glossary 85
Additional Reading 87
Index 89

Introduction

Walking through the streets of modern-day Boston, it's impossible not to notice the parallel red lines painted on the city's sidewalks, linking diverse neighborhoods including Government Center, Beacon Hill, and the North End. Boston's Freedom Trail, a connection of sixteen sites spread over 2.5 miles, tells the story of the American Revolution, keeps the voices of the people behind the peril and victory alive, and unravels the truth behind one of American's most historical cities. From Faneuil Hall, the site of heated debates, to the Old North Church, made famous on the night of Paul Revere's Ride, to the Charlestown-docked USS *Constitution,* a survivor of multiple battles and the War of 1812, each designated stop is not only steeped in history but alive with the spirit that led to our country's independence. It's here, in the "Hub," as the city is affectionately and appropriately known, that the central fight for freedom took place.

Once inhabited by Algonquin tribes, the Shawmut Peninsula is the land on which the city of Boston was built. William Blackstone is said to have been the first man of European descent to live in the area, and was the sole resident of what later became the Boston Common. (He sold his land to the

Faneuil Hall as depicted in 1789.

Massachusetts Government in 1634.) John Winthrop and Puritan settlers landed in Salem and then took on the task of building what Winthrop deemed the "City on the Hill." Puritan values ruled the city and all facets of everyday life.

The Revolution That Shaped the City

A hundred years later, Boston was the location for key events in the American Revolution. The Colonies rejection of British rule manifested itself in debates, rebellions, and eventually, bloody battles and causalities on both sides. From

Engraving of British ships bringing troops in 1768 to Boston by Paul Revere (done 1770).

BOSTON 1600 — 1700

1630 John Winthrop arrives with Puritans in Salem.

King's Chapel Burying Ground established (the oldest cemetery in Boston).

1634 William Blackstone sells what becomes Boston Common to the Massachusetts government.

1635 Boston Latin School established.

1636 Harvard University established.

1659 Copp's Hill Burying Ground established.

1660 Granary Burying Ground established.

1710 King's Chapel rebuilt (replacing original wooden structure).

1' Old S House b

Charlestown burned on the day of the Battle of Bunker Hill.

the rejection of taxes on tea to the dispute over unwarranted searches, Patriot leaders including Paul Revere, John Adams, and John Hancock emerged and Boston became a hotbed of political activity and rebellion. Local government solidified and the foundation for this leading New England city, a place revered for its educational institutions and literary legacies, was set.

While every day of the Revolution (mid 1760s–mid 1780s) was significant, specific events stand out as monumental in the fight for freedom. On March 5, 1770, the Boston Massacre was the conflict's first bloodshed. The aftermath of the deaths of five Patriots, killed in confusion on a dark night, and the resulting accusation and trial of the British soldiers (represented in court by John Adams) shaped the years that followed. Three years later the famous

1723 d North ch built.

1729 Old South Meeting House built.

1734 Paul Revere born.

1742 Faneuil Hall opens.

1764 Sugar Tax enacted.

1765 Stamp Act enacted.

1766 Stamp Act repealed.

1767 Townsend Acts.

1768 British troops form encampment on Boston Common.

Massachusetts Circular Letter written by Samuel Adams.

Bird's-eye view of Boston, circa 1870s.

Boston Tea Party took place. On December 16, 1773, colonists dressed as Native Americans dumped tea in the harbor in defiance of the British-imposed Tea Act. This dramatic rebellion lives on in the city through annual reenactments. While most schoolchildren know the date April 18, 1775, as Paul Revere's Midnight Ride, the significance of Revere's legendary night was anything but elementary and would change the face of the city. Only two months later, on June 17, 1775, at the Battle of Bunker Hill, significant bloodshed (on the American and British sides) took place. The people, places and voices behind these events, as well as the everyday fight for freedom, is a rich and complex part of American history that unfolds on the Freedom Trail.

March 5, 1770 Boston Massacre takes place.

1773 Tea Act enacted.

December 16, 1773 Boston Tea Party.

1774 Closing of the port.

April 18, 1775 Paul Revere's Midnight Ride.

June 17, 1775 Battle of Bunker Hill.

1776 The British evacuate Boston.

July 8, 1776 Declaration of Independence is read for the first time in Boston from the Old State House balcony.

1780 John Hancock becomes the first governor of the Commonwealth of Massachusetts.

1789 George Washington becomes first president of the United States.

1794–179 USS *Constitu-tion* ("O Ironsides bui

Story of the Trail

The sixteen sites of the Freedom Trail: Boston Common, the Massachusetts State House, Park Street Church, Granary Burying Ground, King's Chapel, the First School Site/Statue of Benjamin Franklin, Old Corner Bookstore, Old South Meeting House, Old State House Museum, Faneuil Hall, Paul Revere's House, Old North Church, Copp's Hill Burying Ground, USS *Constitution,* and the Monument at Bunker Hill all tell a different piece of the story of the formation of the city, but their history is unequivocally intertwined. Even so, it wasn't until 1951 that the formal idea of a trail, linking each site with designated signage, came to fruition. Credited to Boston journalist William Schofield, the trail was inspired by Schofield's own confusion in attempting to find each historic site. He wondered how visitors could escape getting lost. Schofield wrote a column for the evening edition of the *Herald Traveler* outlining a plan for the trail and asking for the help of local businessmen and then-mayor John B. Hynes. In June 1951, the trail was born and attracts thousands of visitors annually. Over the next several years, organization improved, and in 1958 the red lines linking the sites were painted. Boston National Historical Park became involved in the mid-'70s and continues to educate and inform the public with free tours of some of the sites and access to well-stocked information centers.

Some of the Freedom Trail sites—including the Park Street Church and Old South Meeting House—were saved throughout the years from demolition and radical changes. Others struggled with the finances for restoration—such as the USS *Constitution*—and were rescued by the hard work and goodwill of the community. Ongoing restoration, careful preservation, and daily

1800

1797 Adams [be]comes second [presi]dent of United States.

1798 Charles Bulfinch completes the "New" Massachusetts State House.

1809 Park Street Church founded.

1816 Paul Revere casts replacement bells for King's Chapel, the largest bells he ever cast.

1824–1826 Quincy Market built.

1832 Publishers Ticknor and Fields purchase the Old Corner Bookstore.

1872 The Great Boston Fire kills 33 people.

1874 Massachusetts State House dome is gilded.

maintenance is critical to these meeting houses, public buildings, churches, cemeteries, and ship. The millions of dollars and uncountable volunteer hours that keep these sites running indicate one thing: Bostonians love their city and honor its past with this unique walk through history.

Beyond the Freedom Trail

While the sixteen sites may comprise the bulk of one's historic tour of Boston, historically significant walks and sites abound. The Black Heritage Trail is a 1.6-mile trail running through Beacon Hill, featuring structures of importance in the pre–Civil War African-American community. Norman B. Leventhal Walk to the Sea begins at the Massachusetts State House and continues on what was originally the harbor, exploring Boston's past in association with the sea. Specific sites off the Freedom Trail that are not to be missed include the New England Holocaust Memorial, in Government Center. It was created in 1995 and is dedicated to the six million Jews killed in the Holocaust. Beacon Hill's Charles Bulfinch–designed Otis House Museum provides an example of Federalist architecture, circa 1796, and how the governing class once lived. Presidential history is preserved at the John F. Kennedy Library and Museum in South Boston.

In this unique city, history even extends itself to the world-class hotels and restaurants. From the historic Omni Parker House—situated downtown, across the street from King's Chapel, the Saturday Literary Club, which counted renowned authors Ralph Waldo Emerson and Nathaniel Hawthorne as members, met in the elegant hotel in the mid-1800s. At the swank, award-winning Liberty Hotel in tony Beacon Hill, a multimillion-dollar renovation took

1900

1888 Memorial for the Boston Massacre erected in Boston Common.

1897 Boston's annual marathon begins

Boston's subway system, the oldest in the country, begins operation.

1902 Subway line built underneath the Old State House.

1951 Freedom Trail invented by journalist William Schofield.

1958 Red lines on Freedom Trail painted.

196 John Kenne becom thirty-fif president the Unite State

place on what was the circa-1851 Charles Street Jail, and the see-and-be-seen restaurant Bond, in the Financial District's refined Langham Hotel, gives a nod to its past as a Federal Reserve Bank (c. 1920) with oversized replications of money bills hanging on the walls.

A Visitor's Journey

The sites on the trail are run by enthusiastic, knowledgeable staff and volunteers who make it a true pleasure to visit. The National Parks Service has done an outstanding job providing information and free tours. Paid, organized tours are also an option and one can supplement information and additional visiting time if desired. The trail is perfectly laid out to venture out with only book in hand. One can pick and choose how long to spend at each site, and arrange the hours that suit a schedule best. While the school year can bring large groups on field trips, the energy and faces of young "historians" can add to the experience. One thing is a must for all travelers: comfortable walking shoes. While some sites are free, others only accept cash (keep it handy). It's a good idea to carry bottled water and plan time for eating and respites. Check rules at each site regarding photography. Hours vary during summer and winter months, so plan accordingly.

Today the Freedom Trail is set against a backdrop of Boston's modern urban life. Bostonian's work days unfold just feet away from museums. Chain stores have popped up in the shadows of historic sites, but whether one has only a day or two or the luxury of a longer stay, it's impossible not to come face to face with the past in this very much alive and thriving city. One may even hear the voices of the past echo through Boston's historic streets.

2000

1989 obert Gould haw Memoal becomes part of the Boston African American National istoric Site.

1991 Big Dig construction project begins.

1995 The New England Holocaust Memorial erected.

2007 Battle of Bunker Hill Museum completed.

2011 Projected completion of USS *Constitution* restoration.

Key Participants

John Adams (1735–1826) Adams served two terms as vice president, and served as the second president of the United States (1797–1801). He was a delegate to the first and second Continental Congresses. A Harvard-trained attorney, Adams agreed to represent the British soldiers accused of murder in the Boston Massacre.

Samuel Adams (1722–1803) Well educated—he attended Boston Latin and Harvard—and from a prosperous family, Adams began his career as a tax collector, yet is best known for his role in the American Revolution. He's often credited with founding the "Sons of Liberty," organized patriots who rebelled against British rule. Adams was responsible for leading the protest against the Stamp Act, and was an organizer of the Boston Tea Party. He is one of the signers of the Declaration of Independence, served in the Massachusetts State Senate, and was elected governor in 1794. He is buried at the Granary Burying Ground.

Charles Bulfinch (1763–1844) The architect of Federal-style Boston homes, churches, and government buildings used knowledge garnered on his European travels to influence his works. Bulfinch's buildings and expansions include the Massachusetts State House, Faneuil Hall, and St. Stephen's Church. The Harvard-educated Bostonian's remains are in the crypt below King's Chapel.

Peter Faneuil (1700–1743) The New York–born wealthy merchant moved to Boston and is best known for his gift of market/town hall Faneuil Hall, which later became known as the "Cradle of Liberty" and was the site of numerous debates, including against the Sugar Tax of 1764 and the Stamp Act of 1765. He is buried at the Granary Burying Ground.

Benjamin Franklin (1706–1790) The Founding Father's history began in Boston. Born in the city, he attended Boston Latin (the famous statue of Franklin is displayed at the school's former site). He was a renowned inventor as well as printmaker, writer, and politician.

John Hancock (1737–1793) Like Samuel Adams, Hancock grew up in a wealthy family and attended Boston Latin and Harvard, and is a signer of the Declaration of Independence. Though today he is best known for his fanciful signature, his true claim to fame is as one of the leaders of the Revolution, protesting British rule. General Gage gave orders to arrest Hancock (along with John Adams) and try him for treason in London. Paul Revere set out to warn the two men on his Midnight Ride. Hancock served as Governor of Massachusetts, and was president of the Continental Congress. He is buried at the Granary Burying Ground.

Robert Newman (1752–1804) Sexton/caretaker for the Old North Church, Patriot Newman became famous for climbing the church tower and holding the two lanterns on April 18, 1775, the night of Paul Revere's Midnight Ride, alerting the Patriots of the British route. Newman is said to have escaped through the church window when British troops stormed the building. He is buried in Copp's Hill Burying Ground.

James Otis Jr. (1725–1783) A Harvard-educated attorney, Otis was a staunch defender of Colonial Rights and was vehemently opposed to and spoke out against the Writs of Assistance. He is said to have coined Faneuil Hall, the "Cradle of Liberty." He had an untimely death, the result of being struck by lightning.

Colonel William Prescott (1726–1795) Colonel Prescott led 1,200 colonial troops to Breed's Hill on June 16, 1775, forming an overnight encampment. He is best known for the command "Don't fire 'til you see the whites of their eyes" given at the next-day's Battle of Bunker Hill. The original monument at Bunker Hill was dedicated solely to Prescott. A statue in his honor is proudly displayed on the grounds.

Paul Revere (1734–1818) A central figure of the American Revolution, Boston-born Revere is most famous for his Midnight Ride of April 18, 1775. He set off for Lexington to warn John Hancock and Samuel Adams of the approaching British. In his long and varied career he was a goldsmith/silversmith (contributing to projects including the USS *Constitution* and the King's Chapel Bell), dentist, illustrator/engraver (he produced the famous Boston Massacre scene), and lieutenant colonel in the Massachusetts State Train Artillery. Revere had two wives and fathered sixteen children. He is buried at the Granary Burying Ground.

Colonel Robert Gould Shaw (1837–1863) The wealthy, Boston-born Shaw led the all-black 54th Regiment to Fort Wagner, South Carolina, on July 18, 1863. He was killed in the Civil War battle. The 54th Regiment was one of the first groups of African-Americans to fight in war. They are honored, along with Shaw, with a bronze relief across from the Massachusetts State House.

Dr. Joseph Warren (1741–1775) A Freemason and Harvard-trained doctor, Dr. Warren was an active leader during the Revolution and is noted for giving two commemorative Boston Massacre speeches. He served as a volunteer and was killed at the Battle of Bunker Hill. The historic Warren Tavern in Charlestown is named in his honor.

John Winthrop (1588–1649) One of the founders of the Massachusetts Bay Colony, English-born Winthrop arrived in Salem in 1630 on the *Arbella* with a group of Puritans with the goal of founding a new colony. He is known for delivering the sermon "A Model of Christian Charity" on the ship. He is buried in the King's Chapel Burying Ground.

Tour Stop 1: Boston Common

A sign marks an entrance to the historic Boston Common.

Boston Common, Bordered by Tremont, Beacon, Charles, Park, and Boylston streets, Boston, MA, www.cityofboston.gov/FreedomTrail/boston common.asp. Always open. Free. BEACON HILL

The start of the Freedom Trail, this bucolic nearly 50-acre outdoor site has a long and rich history not apparent from the casual activities that take place here today—children playing, families on a leisurely weekend strolls, downtown workers taking relaxing lunch breaks. The Common is touted as the oldest park in the country. Its origins are traced back to Boston settler and clergyman William Blackstone, who sold the land to the Massachusetts Government in 1634. The town initially used the space as a common grazing area for cattle and livestock, and Boston households were charged six schillings for the government's purchase. The idea for the Common was carried over from the Puritans' idea of common land set aside for the use of the townspeople. The size and overall setup of the Common hasn't changed over the years, but documentation shows it originally included three ponds and four hills. Today only one pond (Frog Pond) one hill (Flagstaff) remain.

While much celebrating has taken place here, the Common also has a dark past. In 1660 the Common was first used for hangings, including that of Mary Dyer, a Puritan turned Quaker. She was arrested for aiding two Quaker friends and exiled. Upon returning to Boston she was arrested again and the mother of six children was executed on June 1, 1660. Executions took place until the

A view from Beacon Hill 1775–1780. The landscape of Boston has changed dramatically over the years.

gallows were removed in 1817. Between 1768 and 1775 British troops (counted at 1,750 men) camped on the Common. They departed from the Common for Lexington and Concord, and for the Battle of Bunker Hill.

In 1830, cattle grazing was prohibited and the park took on a recreational focus and became a gathering place for monumental events. The Common has been the site of various protests and gatherings through the years, including antislavery protests during the Civil War. Among the notable figures who have spoken here over the years are George Whitefield, Martin Luther King Jr., Pope John Paul II, Gloria Steinem, and President Barack Obama.

It is here that on August 27, 1862, at the Mass Meeting in Aid of Recruitment, Representative and one-time Speaker of the House Robert Charles Winthrop gave his "A Star for Every State, and a State for Every Star" speech:

> *It is a time when every one of us should ask himself, day by day, and night by night, at morning, and at evening, and at noonday, "What can I say, or what can I do, for my country, and for those who are engaged in its defence?" Yet I cannot help feeling how powerless are any mere empty words in presence of such events as those which have called us together. The rolling drum, the pealing*

View of Boston Common in 1910.

bells, the tramp of marching battalions, the shouts of surging multitudes—these are the only sounds to-day which seem to fill or satisfy the ear; and the only adequate words which the vocabulary of American Patriotism can supply for such an hour as this are, "Recruit, enlist, gird on your armor and go forth to the rescue of our brethren in the field, and to the deliverance of our beloved country."

A **Freedom Trail Information Center** is located on the Tremont Street side (open Mon–Sat 8:30–5, Sun 9–5). Those following the Freedom Trail may find it convenient to enter the Common at Tremont Street and Park Street. Here, you'll find the entrance to the Park Street subway station (the T), the oldest subway line in the U.S. Boston's subway began with an open-bench four-wheel trolley car, and made its first run at 6:02 a.m. on September 1, 1897, carrying 175 passengers. The trolley ran along Park and Boylston streets.

A short walk (towards Beacon Street) brings visitors to family-friendly **Frog Pond** where in 1848 the 90-foot water fountain was added and what was once considered a small water hole was expanded into a man-made lake. Ice skating takes place on the pond November–mid-March (Mon–Fri 10–5, Tues–Thurs and Sun 10–9, Sat 10–10; $4, children under 13 free; skate rental $8, children

13 and under $5). A snack bar and carousel (daily 11–9; $3) are located here.

Viewable from Frog Pond is a circle of benches surrounded by tall trees. At the center is the Soldiers and Sailors Monument created by Martin Millmore in 1877. A memorial for the Civil War, the gray monument, set atop three steps, consists of carved wreaths and reliefs depicting the Civil War period. The monument was built on Flagstaff Hill.

Other notable sites in the Common include the Boston Massacre Memorial created in 1888 by Robert Kraus, and the Central Burying Ground, dating back to 1756.

"To the men of Boston who died for their country on land and sea in the war which kept the union whole destroyed slavery and maintained the constitution the grateful city has build this monument that their example may speak to coming generations."

—Engraved on the Soldiers and Sailors Monument

Erected in 1888, The Boston Massacre Monument is a not-to-be missed site in Boston Common.

The Robert Gould Shaw Memorial became part of the Boston African American Historical Society in 1989.

Before heading to the second tour stop, the Massachusetts State House, reserve time to view the **Robert Gould Shaw Memorial,** directly across the street from the State House and fourteen steps up from the Common, on Beacon Street. Created by Augustus Saint-Gaudens (1848–1907), this striking bronze depiction of gun-toting soldiers and an officer on horseback, honors Colonel Robert Gould Shaw and members of the 54th Massachusetts Regiment who died in the assault on Fort Wagner, South Carolina, on July 18th, 1863. The unit was the first in the Civil War to be comprised of black soldiers. The memorial became part of the Boston African American National Historic Site in 1989.

Tour Stop 2: Massachusetts State House

Massachusetts State House, Corner of Beacon and Park streets, Boston, MA, (617) 727-3676, www.sec.state.ma.us/trs/trsidx.htm. Mon–Fri 10–4; guided 45-minute tours by reservation throughout the day. Free. BEACON HILL

This impressive redbrick-edifice Federalist-style building with Doric columns that is the site of much government hustle and bustle was once John Hancock's cow pasture. Completed in 1798, the original structure, designed by Charles Bulfinch, was significantly smaller (set on a 1.6-acre lot) than today's building, (set on a 6.7-acre lot). Perched on the south summit of Beacon Hill, across the street from the Boston Common, this is the oldest building in Beacon Hill's historic neighborhood.

This Federalist-style building was designed by Charles Bulfinch and later expanded.

The easy-to-spot red line running through the city lets visitors know they are on the Freedom Trail.

After the American Revolution, the desire for a larger, independent space was expressed, and the Old State House's operations were moved to the Bulfinch building (often referred to as the New State House) on January 11, 1798. The striking gold dome was originally covered in wood shingles and whitewashed. In 1802, to prevent leaking, it was covered in copper sheeting by Paul Revere and Sons. It was gilded in 23-karat gold leaf in 1874, at a cost of $2,862.50. The gilding is replaced every twenty years and in 1997, ran a bill of $300,000. The dome was painted black during World War II for fear it would reflect light during blackouts and be bombed. The pinecone atop the dome is a symbol of the importance of lumber companies.

The steps (to the left of the visitor entrance) are reserved for three special occasions: presidential visits (William Howard Taft made the last official visit in 1912), the departing of governors, and the return of Massachusetts's regimental flags.

Self-guided as well as volunteer-guide-led tours begin on the second floor, in the Doric Hall (named for the columns in the room). Enter the building on Beacon Street (near the statue of General Hooker), pass through security, turn left and proceed to the elevator and take it one floor up. During peak months and hours, expect large groups of schoolchildren. The first stop is Nurses Hall, featuring a memorial statue of a Civil War nurse by Bela Pratt (1914). Three significant scenes are depicted in the hanging paintings: the Midnight Ride of Paul Revere, James Otis arguing against the Writs of Assistance, the Boston Tea Party. This section of the building was an addition made in 1895, as part of an expansion designed by Charles Brigham.

Massachusetts soldiers are honored in the circular room known as the Hall of Flags.

Amidst the marble columns are images of some of the flags Massachusetts soldiers carried to battle dating from the Civil War to the Vietnam War. The seals of the original thirteen colonies are depicted on the stained glass skylight. It's in this room Henry Walker's mural of the pilgrims first seeing land is depicted.

Portraits of governors line the Memorial Hall Gallery on this floor.

The third floor is home to the House of Representatives, Senate, and the Executive chambers. Small wooden desks dating back to the 1800s (signs of their age are evident by the covered ink wells), with more recently implemented "yea" and "nay" buttons, dominate the chamber of the House of Representatives, where the 160 state representatives (elected for two-year terms) meet and vote. The names of fifty-three men (no women are represented) who helped shaped history are listed on the base of the dome in this room and include John Adams and Benjamin Franklin. The most famous aspect of the room is the Sacred Cod, a wooden fish presented to the house by merchant John Rowe.

The Senate Chamber, part of the original Bulfinch design, is under the gold dome and is the oldest section of State House. It's here forty state senators meet around a wooden table in gold leather chairs adjusted based on each senator's height, so they all see eye to eye. Two hundred years ago, the room was filled with bleacher seating. Senators vote by voice in the Tiffany-blue room, decorated with busts including George Washington, Abraham

A pedestrian walks past the gates of King's Chapel Burying Ground on Tremont Street.

"I stand before you as a moral being, endowed with precious and unalienable rights, which are correlative with solemn duties and high responsibilities; and as a moral being I feel that I owe it to the suffering slave, and to the deluded master, to my country and my world to do all that I can to overturn a system of complicated crimes, built up upon the broken hearts and prostrate bodies of my countrymen in chains, and cemented by the blood and sweat and tears of my sisters in bonds."

—Angelina Grimke, February 21, 1838

Lincoln, and the only non-American, Marquis de Lafayette, who laid the cornerstone for the Bunker Hill Monument in 1825. The first British gun captured during the Revolution is on display in the room, and as part of the chandelier is a brass cod, known as the "Holy Mackerel," said to have been given to the Senate after the Sacred Cod was moved from the chamber when the Representatives (who used to meet in this space) moved in 1895. In this room in 1838 Angelina Grimke, an advocator of women's right's and abolitionist, became the first woman to address a U.S. legislative body.

The Executive offices, housing the current governor's office, are also located on the third floor, and feature a waiting room with recent governor's portraits.

Outside the State House, historical figures are honored. Seven statues can be found on the grounds: of John F. Kennedy, Joseph Hooker, Henry Cabot Lodge, Daniel Webster, Horace Mann, Anne Hutchinson, and Mary Dyer.

Tour Stop 3: Park Street Church

Park Street Church, One Park Street, Boston, MA, (617) 523-3383, www.parkstreet.org. June 19–Aug 29, Tues–Fri 9–4, Sat 9–3; open at other times by appointment. Guided tours available. Free. BEACON HILL

The year 2009 marked the bicentennial of this church that was founded by twenty-six members who created the Religious Improvement Society—most of whom belonged to the Old South Church. This Evangelical church sprung from a group of devout Christians in a time of growing liberal ideas of Unitarianism in the city.

The year 2009 marked the Bicentennial of the Park Street Church.

"I call upon the ambassadors of Christ everywhere to make known the proclamation: 'Thus saith the Lord God of the Africans, Let this people go that they may serve me.' I ask them to 'proclaim liberty to the captives, and the opening of the prison to them that are bound'—to light up a flame of philanthropy that shall burn till all Africa be redeemed from the night of moral death, and the song of deliverance be heard throughout her borders. I call upon the churches of the living God to lead this great enterprise."

—July 4, 1829, William Lloyd Garrison, Park Street Church pulpit. Excerpt of his speech "Dangers of the Nation."

The church was built for a total cost of $70,000 on the corner of Park and Tremont streets, next to the Granary Burying Ground. The Granary building was torn down to make room for the Peter Banner–designed church (based on a Christopher Wren design) featuring a striking 217-foot steeple and wooden column capitals carved by Solomon Willard, the architect of the Bunker Hill Monument.

The interior of the church is Puritan, featuring a pulpit as a center focal point. While today one sees row pews, the church was originally outfitted with box pews. It's been said that brimstone (sulfur), used to make gunpowder, was stored in a crypt in the basement for the War of 1812 and hence the church became known as "Brimstone Corner."

The church calls itself "a church of firsts" and it is indeed here that momentous happenings took place for the first time, including on July 4, 1829, when abolitionist and publisher of *The Liberator,* an anti-slavery newspaper, William Lloyd Garrison gave his first public anti-slavery speech on a rainy day to what's been described as a "sizeable" crowd.

Two years later on Independence Day, the first singing of Samuel Francis Smith's hymn, "America" (performed by the Park Street Church Children's Choir) took place on the church steps. The oldest radio ministry in the U.S. began here in 1923. Significant societies have also begun within the church walls, including American's first prison ministry, the first U.S. animal humane society, the American Temperance Society, and the Boston Chapter of the NAACP.

On December 9, 1902, news was announced that the Park Street Church was being sold with

the plans to tear down and build an office building. An offer for $1,250,000 was accepted, causing a public outrage over the destruction of what was already considered a landmark. Meetings and hearings took place and papers throughout the country expressed opposition.

The historic building was preserved and today the church boasts a large congregation—nearly 2,000 come to worship on the weekend, as well as over 50,000 Freedom Trail visitors annually. The church hosts a variety of outings, lectures, concerts, and other events.

"Another Boston landmark gone! Another historic shrine to be razed to the ground! Time and modern Progress to be subserved, but particularly for the latter; for Park Street Church which sits so quaintly where Tremont crosses the foot of Beacon Hill, has been sold.

A celebrated corner, truly. The famous Boston Common spreads away to the southward, and the frogs on summer days send aquatic music up from the pond where Gage's "redcoats" taunted the patriotic lads of 1775 by marring their skating-ground, till the British leader, admiring their spirit, orders the soldiers to desist. On the north the church shadows fling their gloom across the decaying slate headstones of Granary Burying-ground, and Old Park Street Church is to give way to a modern 'sky-scraper.'"

—From the article "Old Park Street Church Sold," which appeared in *The Maroon,* Chicago.

Tour Stop 4: Granary Burying Ground

Granary Burying Ground, Tremont Street (at Bromfield Street), Boston, MA, www.cityofboston.gov/freedomtrail/granary.asp. Daily 9–5. Free. BEACON HILL

Once part of the Boston Common (now separated by Park Street), this shady area was originally called South Burying Ground because it was in the southernmost part of Boston settlement. Boston expanded and the grounds were renamed Middle Ground. Eventually, it became known as the Granary because grain was stored where the Park Street Church stands today.

Situated in a thriving part of the city—where Beacon Hill meets Downtown—the Suffolk

Over 5,000 people have been laid to rest in the Granary Burying Ground.

Miniature flags wave at the Samuel Adams Grave in the Granary Burying Ground.

University Law School has a main building directly across the street from the Egyptian Revival gates that lead into the burying grounds. These gates were designed by Isaiah Rogers, an architect known for his hotels who created almost identical gates for the Touro cemetery in Newport, Rhode Island.

Established in 1660, this is the third oldest cemetery in the city (after King's Chapel and Copp's Hill) and home to over 5,000 bodies, though only 2,300 markers. For economic reasons, headstones weren't always placed with each body. It's here that Samuel Adams, John Hancock, Paul Revere, James Otis, Peter Faneuil, the five victims of the Boston Massacre, and the parents of Benjamin Franklin are laid to rest.

The most visited site in the grounds is the memorial and small grave of Paul Revere at the north side. Coins placed on top of the memorial are a sign of respect for the metalsmith and Patriot who rests underneath the shady trees in the city where he became famous.

Tour Stop 5: King's Chapel

King's Chapel, Corner of School and Tremont streets, Boston, MA, (617) 227-2155, www.kings-chapel.org. Year-round, Sat 10–4 and Sun 1:30–4; July and Aug, daily 10–4; introductory tours Wed at noon; check Web site for concert schedule. (Due to ongoing restoration work, call to confirm hours.) $1 suggested donation. DOWNTOWN

If one were to stand at the corner of School and Tremont streets in 1688, one would see a small wooden structure built on Puritan burial land for the first Anglican congregation in New England, established two years prior. In 1710, the wooden structure was rebuilt and doubled in size. It wasn't until nearly four decades later (1749–1754) that the sturdy Quincy granite building, anchoring what is now a bustling downtown corner, was built. The

Originally built as a wooden structure, King's Chapel was rebuilt with Quincy granite in 1710, and doubled in size.

Georgian-style chapel, designed by Peter Harrison, was constructed around the wooden chapel, and once completed, the wooden pieces were taken apart and removed through the windows of the current structure. Harrison's plans for a steeple were never carried out due to lack of funds, yet the building is topped with a historic gem. The sound of the bell that rings on Sunday mornings as modern-day Bostonians hustle to brunch, and scurry down Tremont, was hung in 1816 and is credited to Paul Revere, who cast the piece, his largest bell, in 1814.

"It was the sweetest bell I ever made."

—Paul Revere (in regard to the King's Chapel Bell he cast in 1816)

Today, the floor of the chapel is still held up by a crypt, part of the original 1686 structure. The crypt is home to the remains of over 100 bodies including those of Charles Bulfinch, Charles Paxton, and Royal Governor William Shirley. Visitors can view the communion table and chancel tablets given to the chapel by King William and Queen Mary in 1696, as well as the 1717 Peter Vintoneau–designed pulpit, the oldest continuously used pulpit (in the same space) in the country, and the Governor's Pew, where in 1778, George Washington sat for an oration.

The chapel was originally named after King James II but after the British evacuated Boston in 1776 it was called "the Stone Chapel," and in March of that year, the chapel was temporarily closed. Unitarian ideas were accepted into the church in 1785 after being introduced by Minister James Freeman, who was denied ordainment by Bishop Seabury. Freeman was later ordained by the Senior Warden of the King's Chapel in 1787, and the chapel is considered the first Unitarian church in the United States. It was renamed King's Chapel in 1789.

The King's Chapel Burying Ground

Once considered the outskirts of the new Puritan settlement, the King's Chapel Burying Ground is the oldest burial ground in Boston. Established in 1630, this small and shady space is home to 600 gravestones and more than two dozen tombs, and it's been estimated that over 1,000 people are buried here. Ironically, aside from proximity (adjacent), the cemetery has no connection with King's Chapel, or in fact, any religious affiliation, and is owned by the city of Boston.

Burials took place here until 1896 and John Winthrop, who arrived with Puritans on the *Arbella*; Mary Chilton, noted as the first European woman to step ashore at Plymouth; Elizabeth Pain, said to be the inspiration for Nathaniel Hawthorne's *The Scarlet Letter*; and William Emerson, the father of Ralph Waldo Emerson, were laid to rest here.

The site has had its fair share of changes. It was first fenced in 1642, changing the cemetery's boundaries, and a series of new fences were constructed for the next two hundred years. In 1896, a subway ventilation shaft was installed in the southwest corner, forcing some remains to be moved to other parts of the grounds. Today, visitors can hear the rumble of the trains beneath their feet.

Established 1630, King's Chapel Burying Ground is the oldest cemetery in Boston.

Tour Stop 6: First Public School/ Statue of Benjamin Franklin

First Public School/Statue of Benjamin Franklin, 45 School Street, Boston, MA, www.cityofboston.gov/freedomtrail/firstpublic.asp. Always open. Free. DOWNTOWN

The lit courtyard of the nationally touted steakhouse Ruth's Chris may seem an unlikely Freedom Trail stop. The area is occupied by Old City Hall,

Benjamin Franklin was born on Boston's Milk Street and later attended Boston Latin.

Old City Hall on School Street as seen in 1903.

which includes the restaurant, but the corner of the property was once the site of the Boston Public Latin School. The mosaic—comprised of ceramic, brass, and glass, and created by artist Lilli Ann Killen Rosenberg in 1983—commemorates the original site of this legendary educational institution.

A mural commemorating the site of the orginal Boston Latin School was completed in 1983 by artist Lilli Ann Killen.

Established April 13, 1635, Boston Latin is the oldest continuously operating public school in the United States (in 1922 the school moved to the Fenway district). The Town of Boston funded the school, first located in the home of schoolmaster Philemon Pormont. The school was run from schoolmasters' homes until 1645 when the schoolhouse was built. Boston Latin credits its beginnings to the influence of Reverend John Cotton, who envisioned the school after the Free Grammar School of Boston, England, and included the teachings of Greek and Latin. Its list of former pupils includes Benjamin Franklin, John Hancock, Samuel Adams, Robert Treat Paine, and William Hopper. All were signers for the Declaration of Independence. Other noteworthy students include Cotton Mather, Samuel Mather, Thomas Hutchinson, Josiah Quincy Jr. (a statue for him is also erected here), Charles Bulfinch, and Ralph Waldo Emerson.

At this site you will also find an 8-foot bronze statue of Benjamin Franklin (1706–1790) dated 1856 by Richard Saltonstall Greenough, and noted as the first portrait statue erected in the city. Franklin, a dropout of Boston Latin, was born at 17 Milk Street (less than two blocks away; no longer standing) and christened at the original Old South Meeting House. Among his many accomplishments he is noted as being one of six men who signed the Declaration of Independence and the Constitution of the United States. He was a strong supporter for the abolition of slavery. Franklin was also a writer and printmaker, as well as a noted inventor.

"This being the only public school in the town for about half a century, it is reasonable to infer that the elementary as well as the higher branches were taught. Its principal objective, however, from its establishment to the present time, has been to prepare young men for college. 'Out of small beginnings,' says Bradford, 'great things have been produced; and as one small candle may light a thousand, so the light here kindled hath shone to many, yea, in some sort, to our whole nation.' He must have had in his mind the first Boston school, which has perpetuated in the present Latin school. Its origin was simple and unpretending; its advantages as an educational institution in its early days hardly to be compared with those of the humblest country school of the present time; and yet what a burning and shining light it has become! For nearly two and a half centuries it has been training states men whose wisdom has guided our nation."

—Charles Knapp Dillaway, headmaster of the Latin School, 1831–1836

Before leaving the site, examine the brass footsteps engraved with elephants reading, STAND IN OPPOSITION, and the brass donkey (a favorite photo op), the recognized symbol of the Democratic Party.

The Donkey, a symbol of the Democratic Party, stands proud at the site of the first Public School.

Tour Stop 7: Old Corner Bookstore

Old Corner Bookstore, 3 School Street, Boston, MA. www.cityofboston.gov/FreedomTrail/old corner.asp. Free. DOWNTOWN

Walking into the charming brick building on the corner of School and Washington streets, just down the block from the Parker Omni House where the Saturday Club, a monthly literary gathering took place, Ralph Waldo Emerson pays a visit to his publisher James ("Jamie") Fields. He runs into Nathaniel Hawthorne and Henry Wadsworth Longfellow, and hours go by as the writers converse.

A thriving literary center starting in the mid-1840s, the Old Corner Bookstore attracted some of the greats who came to converse, socialize, and do business. Built on the site of the Anne

The Old Corner Bookstore attracted the literary elite, including Nathaniel Hawthorne.

Hutchinson House (built in 1634 and destroyed by a fire in 1711), the brick structure, featuring an English garden wall bond pattern, was built in 1718 by Dr. Thomas Crease, who used the space as an apothecary and residence. In 1829, Carter & Hendlee were the first of ten bookseller/publishers to use the space. In 1832 Ticknor and Fields purchased the building and a thriving literary scene emerged. The company's authors included Mark Twain, Harriet Beecher Stowe, and Henry David Thoreau, and the company became the publishers of the *Atlantic Monthly* and the *North American Review.* In the 1950s the building fell into disrepair. Saved from demolition, the building was restored in the 1960s and the *Boston Globe* ran offices out of the space. Today, one is more likely to find a Charles Winston diamond ring featured in the window (it's occupied by Direct Diamond Imports) than literary masterpieces, but perhaps it's only fitting that a large Border's bookstore looms across the way, a token reminder to all who pass here that this was once one of the thriving cities for the written word.

Tour Stop 8: Old South Meeting House

Old South Meeting House, 310 Washington Street, Boston, MA. (617) 482-6439, www.oldsouthmeetinghouse.org. Apr–Oct, daily 9:30–5; Nov–Mar, daily 10–4. Adults $5, seniors and students $4; admission includes audio headset use. BEACON HILL

The Old South Meeting House is topped with a 183-foot steeple.

What began as a 51-foot-wide cedar meeting-house for the Third Church of Boston (a group that disagreed with the ideologies of the First Church of Boston and formed a more liberal congregation) quickly outgrew its space on Washington Street. The cedar house, built on the site of John Winthrop's garden, was torn down in 1729, and that same year the austere and beautiful Puritan meeting house, known as the Old South Meeting House, was built. At the time, it was the largest building in Boston. Built of brick in a Flemish bond pattern, the sturdy building is without excess decoration, featuring a white-painted interior and basic wooden floors to reflect the Puritan aesthetic of simplicity and the belief that elaborate decoration would interfere with one's relationship with God. The original (built c.1770) 183-foot steeple remains today.

When used as a church, the downstairs and first gallery of the meetinghouse was reserved for the wealthy and those who paid for use of their pews. Servants and slaves were relegated the free bench seating on the top floor. Though the space was most certainly a place of worship, the Puritans did not consider it sacred and the meetinghouse quickly became known as a place for political and social debate and was used when town meetings at Faneuil Hall became overcrowded. This is exactly what happened on one of the most significant nights in U.S. history.

On December 16, 1773, a chilly night, more than 5,000 colonists pushed into the Old South Meeting House to debate the tax on tea. British Parliament passed a tea tax on May 10, 1773. Tea would be sold in the colonies for low prices, but

"On the day preceding the seventeenth, there was a meeting of the citizens of the county of Suffolk, convened at one of the churches in Boston, for the purpose of consulting on what measures might be considered expedient to prevent the landing of the tea, or secure the people from the collection of the duty. At that meeting a committee was appointed to wait on Governor Hutchinson, and request him to inform them whether he would take any measures to satisfy the people on the object of the meeting. To the first application of this committee, the Governor told them he would give them a definite answer by five o'clock in the afternoon. At the hour appointed, the committee again repaired to the Governor's house, and on inquiry found he had gone to his country seat at Milton, a distance of about six miles. When the committee returned and informed the meeting of the absence of the Governor, there was a confused murmur among the members, and the meeting was immediately dissolved, many of them crying out, "Let every man do his duty, and be true to his country"; and there was a general huzza for Griffin's wharf."

—Account from George Hewes, one of the men and last survivors who took part in the dumping of the tea.

sold only by Loyalists and essentially designed as a scheme for the British to collect revenue from the Americas. On November 28, 1773, a shipment of tea arrived in Boston Harbor. The deadline for the tea tax to be paid was midnight, December 16. Meetings and protests led up to the night of December 16, and on that evening, at the South Meeting House, Samuel Adams exclaimed, "This meeting can do no more to save the Country!" That simple phrase was the signal for the Sons of Liberty to head to the no-longer-present Griffin's Wharf and dump tea into the Boston Harbor. There the colonists threw 342 containers consisting of 90,000 pounds of tea into the water.

Other significant meetings at Old South included the annual commemoration of the Boston Massacre (held 1771–1775) and the protests of the 1774 closing of the port.

In 1775, the British took over the space and used it as a riding school, allowing horses in the building and destroying pews and burning the wood. It was almost a decade later before the church had money to restore the desecrated space. The building narrowly escaped the Great Boston Fire in 1872 and shortly after, even though it was used as an active place of worship, the building was auctioned and put up for lease/sale. A group that included writers Louisa May Alcott, Ralph Emerson, and Henry Wadsworth Longfellow rallied and raised money to save the church. It was spared the wrecking ball and opened as a museum to the public in 1877.

Over a hundred and fifty years after the American Revolution, the walls that had heard much discussion and debate were alive again when the issue of free speech was called for a vote by the board of the Old South. In 1929 it was decided that speakers would be heard here regardless of the popularity of their cause.

Heated voices still take center stage here today. School groups and an organized annual Boston Tea Party Reenactment bring the voices of yesteryear to life. In addition to organized "debates," the meetinghouse is an interactive space, chock-full of educational kiosks examining the issues of the American Revolution and with a diorama of the town of Boston in 1773, as well as a detailed timeline of events. Figures of James Michael Curley, Margaret Sanger, and George Robert Twelves Hewes can be found on the main floor.

The balcony is closed to visitors. Once completing a self-guided tour of the main floor, exit the rear of the room and proceed down the winding, creaky wooden stairs. Here you'll find restrooms and a large gift shop stocked with old-fashioned candy (including Boston Baked Beans), books, CDs, and toys. Outside near the front entrance of the meetinghouse, Lambert's Marketplace sells fresh produce.

Lambert's Marketplace sells fresh produce in front of the Old South Meeting House.

Tour Stop 9: Old State House Museum

Old State House Museum, 206 Washington Street, Boston, MA, (617) 720-1713, www.bostonhistory.org. Jan daily 9–4; Feb–June and Sept–Dec, daily 9–5; July and Aug, daily 9–6. Adults $7, students and seniors $6, ages 6–18 $3, children under 5 free. DOWNTOWN

On the afternoon of July 18, 1776, an exuberant crowd gathers outside the Old State House.

Now a museum, the Old State House glows downtown.

Sons of Liberty member Colonel Thomas Crafts Jr. stands on the east-side balcony, overlooking the site of the Boston Massacre, which took place six years earlier. Facing King Street, he reads the Declaration of Independence for the first time in Boston. Canons are fired, toasts are made, and bells rung. That evening, after this monumental reading and celebrating, all royal emblems, including the now-restored lion and unicorn on the east-end pediment symbolizing British rule, are torn down and burned in a public bonfire to the delight of participants and onlookers.

"Great attention was given to Colonel Kraft's every word. As soon as he ended . . . , three cheers rended the air. . . . Thus ends royal authority in this state, and all the people shall say Amen."

—Abigail Adams, in a letter to her husband

Crowds still gather here for a reading of the Declaration. On the Fourth of July each year, Bostonians come together to celebrate American's independence and listen to the words that created the foundation of America. A historical irony, on July 4, 1976, Queen Elizabeth II stood from this same balcony and addressed an accepting crowd.

"If Paul Revere, Samuel Adams, and other patriots could have known that one day a British monarch would stand on the balcony of the Old State House, from which the Declaration of Independence was first read to the people of Boston, and be greeted in such kind and generous words . . . well, I think they would have been extremely surprised! But perhaps they would also have been pleased to know that eventually we came together again as free peoples and friends to defend together the very ideals for which the American Revolution was fought."

—Queen Elizabeth II, July 4, 1976

Built in 1713, on the site of what was called the "Town House" (a wooden structure destroyed in the Great Fire of 1711), the Old State House (called names including the "Second Town House") was rebuilt in brick and is the oldest surviving building of the British colonies, and the oldest public building in Boston. Before the Revolution, the building was the seat of colonial government. This was the site of the state capitol until 1798, used for commercial purposes from 1799 to 1828, as a City Hall from 1830 to 1841, and once again used as a commercial site from 1841 to 1881. Today, it houses the Boston Society's museum.

A free audio guide tour is available on personal cell phones (dial 617-960-8945). Self-guided tours begin on the gift shop level and include an ongoing

History Channel video entitled *Preserving Boston's Old State House,* providing a good overview of the history of the building and its restoration. On the same level, exhibits feature the Boston Massacre, the British siege of Bunker Hill, and a two-minute audio recording from July 21, 1776, of Abigail Adams' "lively account of festivities surrounding the reading of Declaration."

Climb nineteen steps up the winding staircase to the top floor for three hands-on-history rooms, all kid-friendly and interactive. The Boston Massacre multimedia room is comprised of a six-minute loop (shown in two-minute intervals) with lights, voices, and audio that tells about the fateful event. The top floor features the Representative Hall. Today, the large room is open and features exhibits from the Boston Society, but the layout once consisted of three chambers with rectangular staircases in between, and was used for meetings for the colonial government. It's in this very hall a motion was passed to create a circular letter—to be written by John Adams—to the other colonial assemblies, the response to the Townsend Act that taxed everyday items (including tea) imported into the colonies.

On the other side of the floor is the Council Chamber, featuring Revolutionary War treasures like the drum used by John Robbins at the Battle of Bunker Hill, and a ship model of the USS *Constitution.* It's here that the Royal Governor would meet with councilors, and later in 1761, where James Otis passionately spoke against the Writs of Assistance (search and seizure without any reason). It's been noted that after Otis's argument, John Adams declared, "then and there the child Independence was born." In October 1765, the Stamp Act Congress was formed, leading to what eventually was a repeal by Great Britain in March 1766.

The Bulfinch State House on Beacon Hill was completed in January 11, 1798, and the House of Representatives used the Representative's Hall in what would become the Old State House for the last time that day.

The building eventually fell into disrepair and in 1875 there was an unusual offer from the city of Chicago to purchase the building (they planned to disassemble it and reconstruct it on the shore of Lake Michigan). The offer was turned down and the Bostonian Society took over the property. In 1902 a subway line was built underneath the building and one can hear the rumble of trains when standing on the first floor. Before heading out, it's worthwhile to make a trip to the lowest level. Here you'll find an exhibit of historical photographs of the city of Boston, a reminder of how things used to be.

These famous words are attributed to John Adams after James Otis spoke against the Writs of Assistance in the Old State House.

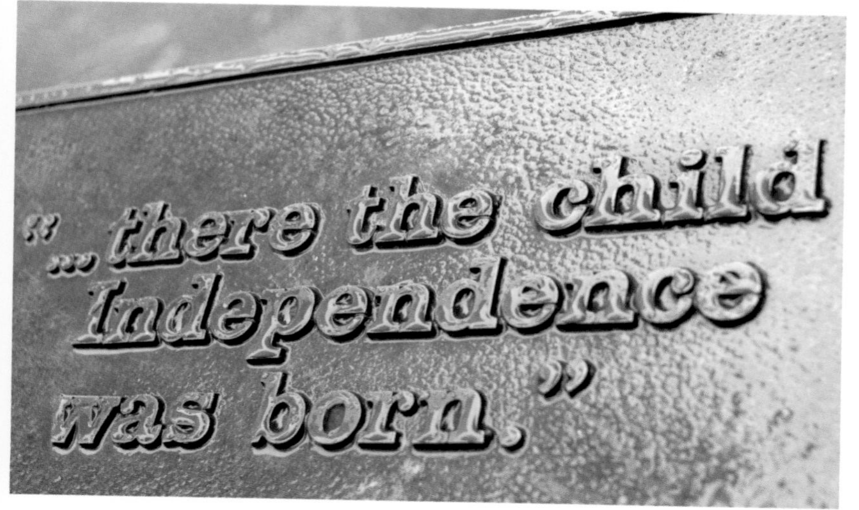

Tour Stop 10: Boston Massacre Site

"The fatal fifth of March 1770, can never be forgotten—The horrors of that dreadful night are but too deeply impressed on our hearts—Language is too feeble to pain the emotions of our souls, when our streets were stained with the blood of our brethren—when our ears were wounded by the groans of the dying and our eyes were tormented with the sight of the mangled bodies of the dead."

—Oration by Dr. Joseph Warren, March 5, 1772, to commemorate March 5, 1770

Boston Massacre Site, Devonshire and State streets, Boston, MA, www.cityofboston.gov/FreedomTrail/bostonmassacre.asp. Always open. Free. DOWNTOWN

March 5, 1770. It was a snowy night, the air was cold. Sometime after 9:00 p.m., a rowdy mob had formed below the Old State House balcony on King Street. It's been said it's here the American Revolution truly began.

Stories of the impetus of the Boston Massacre vary and include reports of an apprentice harassing a British sentry; a young boy mocking a lone sentry; a dispute between a British officer and a wig-maker over an unpaid debt; and a group of angry colonists armed with clubs harassing British troupes. Whatever the case, tensions had been mounting between the colonists and soldiers since the British occupation in 1768 to enforce taxes through the Townsend Acts. It's estimated fifty to seventy-five Bostonians threw rocks, garbage, snow, and coal at British soldiers on the night of March 5, 1770. The crowd swelled and the British troops faced an angry mob. Some historians say an order to fire was called from Captain Thomas Preston, others say it was "Don't fire!" and the message was misheard among the noise of the crowd. One thing is certain: This dark night ended in bloodshed, the first of the American Revolution. Six civilians were wounded, five killed. The men who died—Crispus Attucks (noted as the first casualty of the Revolution), James Caldwell, Samuel Gray, Samuel Maverick, and Patrick Carr—are buried at the Granary Burying Ground.

Opposite page: It's here the first shots of the Revolution were fired on March 5, 1770.

Twenty-one days after the event, what became one of Paul Revere's most famous works, "The Bloody Massacre Perpetrated in King Street," an engraving (which many say is based on a drawing by Henry Pelham) of a line of British soldiers firing at unarmed Bostonians, was sold in prints. The piece is said to have misrepresented the scene, deliberately omitting the chaos and rioting on the part of the colonists, and quickly circulated as a piece of anti-British propaganda.

"The Part I took in Defence of Cptn. Preston and the Soldiers, procured me Anxiety, and Obloquy enough. It was, however, one of the most gallant, generous, manly and disinterested Actions of my whole Life, and one of the best Pieces of Service I ever rendered my Country. Judgment of Death against those Soldiers would have been as foul a Stain upon this Country as the Executions of the Quakers or Witches, anciently. As the Evidence was, the Verdict of the Jury was exactly right."

—From Adams, John. *Diary and Autobiography of John Adams.*

Captain Preston and eight British soldiers were arrested and tried. John Adams was asked to represent the accused and though he had doubts—fearing for his safety and that of his family, along with his reputation, and believing that all deserve a fair defense—he took the case. On March 13, 1770, Preston and the eight soldiers were indicted for murder. On September 7 the men pleaded not guilty. In October through November of that year Preston and the soldiers were tried. All but two soldiers were acquitted of manslaughter. The two were punished by branding of the thumb.

Today the site of that fateful day is a busy intersection, and all that marks the spot is a circle of stones and a small Freedom Trail maker, but the event lives large for Bostonians and those who visit. Each year a reenactment takes place on March 5 in front of the Old State House, and a memorial was erected in Boston Common in 1888.

Tour Stop 11: Faneuil Hall

Faneuil Hall, Congress Street (Dock Square), Boston, MA, (617) 523-1300, www.faneuilhallmarketplace.com. Daily 9–5; historical talks in the Great Hall (2nd floor every half hour 9:30–4:30 (note: if there are only a few visitors, the talks are more informal and a chance to speak one-on-one with a guide). Free. GOVERNMENT CENTER

Perhaps it's only fitting that when Faneuil Hall opened September 10, 1742, it was the product of much controversy and debate. The two-story Georgian-style building designed by John Smibert, built on landfill—the Boston's Harbor shoreline, circa 1630, is engraved outside the front entrance—was the result of wealthy merchant Peter Faneuil's vision for a central food marketplace. A central marketplace had been previously proposed and rejected, and Faneuil's plans to finance the building were accepted by only seven votes (Bostonians voted 367 to 360). Some speculate that the inclusion of a meeting space in the building was to appease those who had been opposed to the marketplace idea, while others cite the Puritan tradition of multipurpose buildings, and a traditional English design with enclosed rooms set above an arcade space. It's also been said that Faneuil had every intention of a dual-purpose building: one part for food, the other for ideas. Whatever the case, in addition to being a marketplace, Faneuil Hall became Boston's first town hall. While produce, meat, and dairy products were being sold in stalls on the first floor, the second floor developed a history rich with verbal

Faneuil Hall opened September 10, 1742. Today it's the site of much hustle and bustle.

sparring, passionate orations, and persuasive speeches.

Though a fire destroyed all but the brick exterior on January 13, 1761, the site known as the "Cradle of Liberty" (James Otis is attributed with coining the name) was really just beginning. It was rebuilt over the next two years to resemble the original structure, and voices of dissent against the British Parliament were heard loud and clear within the walls. Patriots, including Samuel Adams—who is honored with a statue at the entrance of the building on Congress Street—used the space to show opposition of the Sugar Tax (1764), Stamp Act (1765), and Tea Act (1773). "The committees of correspondence" in the colonies were the result of a meeting held in the Great Hall space in 1772.

In the early 1800s, Charles Bulfinch was given the unusual accommodation of free reign with a design to expand the building—the popular space had been outgrown, and in some cases the Old State Meeting House acted as an additional place for debates. The result of Bulfinch's new design was a structure more than double the size of the original, with a third floor. The famous copper weathervane grasshopper that Faneuil had made was retained and still tops the building today.

Even after the Revolution, Faneuil Hall remained a center for important debate and changes. The Anti-Slavery Bazaars were held here from the 1830s to 1840, and in 1903, the Women's Trade Union was founded in the space. The building has also been the site of Massachusetts primary debates. The building underwent major restoration in 1898 and 1992.

The first floor is still used as a marketplace and is filled with kiosks selling Red Sox memorabilia, postcards, old-fashioned candy, and gourmet coffee. A sign reminds visitors that painted stall numbers and meat hooks are remnants from earlier shop days. A working post office is at the Congress Street side of the building and the National Historical Park has a kiosk with free maps and information at the rear. Exit the rear doors and renter the middle doors on the same side (facing Quincy Market) for the staircase to get to the second-floor Great Hall level (restrooms are located on this floor). An elevator in the marketplace is available.

Though the Great Hall is primarily used for historical talks and special events like job fairs, lively discussion still takes place on canvas. Boston-born George Peter Alexander (G.P.A.) Healy's (1813–1894) massive painting *Webster's Reply to Hayne* illustrates Daniel Webster on the Senate floor defending the Union and includes figures such as John C. Calhoun, Judge Sprague, Colonel Washington, John Q. Adams, Mr. Longfellow, John Tyler, William H. Prescott, and Mrs. Webster.

At the bottom of the painting are busts of Lucy Stone (suffragate 1818–1893), Daniel Webster (done by J.C. King, 1850), John Adams (done by M.J. Binen, 1818), Frederick Douglas (1818–1895), and John Quincy Adams (by J.C. King, 1861). The Great Hall also includes reproductions of historical maps of Boston as seen in 1722, 1769, and 1775. Portraits of Robert Treat Paine, Commodore Preble, Samuel Adams, John Hancock, Rufus Choate, and Caleb Strong are on display in the room.

A small alcove on the second floor includes historical information about the building as well as an exhibit of small artifacts recovered during an excavation before a new elevator shaft was dug for the building. The top floors of the building are home to the Ancient and Honorable Artillery Company of Massachusetts (the third-oldest militia in the world) headquarters, and a museum open Monday–Friday 9:00—3:30 (closed Saturday and Sunday).

Tour Stop 12: Paul Revere House

Paul Revere House, 19 North Square, Boston, MA, (617) 523-2338, www.paulreverehouse.org. Apr 15–Oct 31, daily 9:30–5:15; Nov 1–Dec 31 and Apr 1–14, daily 9:30–4:15; Jan–Mar, Tues–Sun 9:30–4:15. Adults $3.50, seniors (62+) and students $3, ages 5–17 $1. NORTH END

The night of April 17, 1775, and Paul Revere is on what will become one of the most famous rides in history. When he returns to the small

The Paul Revere House stands in Boston's North End, close to where the famous silversmith worked.

Paul Revere's Account of his Midnight Ride

Paul Revere of Boston, in the Colony of Massachusetts Bay in New England; of Lawfull Age, doth testify and say, that I was sent for by Docr Joseph Warren, of said Boston, on the evening of the 18th of April, about 10 oClock; when he desired me "to go to Lexington, and inform Mr Samual Adams, and the Honle John Hancock Esqr that there was a number of Soldiers, composed of Light troops, & Grenadiers, marching to the bottom of the Common, where was a number of Boats to receive them; it was supposed, that they were going to Lexington, by the way of Cambridge River, to take them or go to Concord, to distroy the Colony Stores." I proceeded immeditely, and was put across Charles River, and landed near Charlestown Battery, I was informed by Richd Devens Esqr that he mett that evening, after Sun sett, Nine Officers of the Ministeral Army, mounted on good Horses, & Armed, going towards Concord; I set off, it was then about 11 oClock, the Moon shone bright. I had got almost over Charlestown Common, toward Cambridge, when I saw two Officers on Horseback, standing under the shade of a Tree, in a narrow part of the roade, I was near enough to see their Holsters, & cockades. one of them Started his horse towards me, the other up the road, as I supposed, to head me should I escape the first. I turned my horse short about, and rid upon a full Gallop for Mistick Road, he followed me about 300 yardes, and finding he could not catch me, returned. I proceeded to Lexington, thro Mistick, and alarmed Mr Adams & Col. Hancock. After I had been there about half an hour Mr Daws arrived, who came from Boston, over the neck; we set off for Concord, & were overtaken by a young Gentm named Prescot, who belonged to Concord, & was going home; when we had got about half way from Lexington to Concord, the other two, stopped at a House to awake the man, I kept along. When I had got about 200 Yards ahead of them, I saw two officers as before. I called to my company to come up, saing here was two of them, (for I had told them what Mr Devens told me, and of my being stoped) in an instant, I saw four of them, who rode up to me, with their pistols in their hands, said G-d d--n you stop, if go an Inch further, you are a dead Man. immed-itly Mr. Prescot came up we attempted to git thro them, but they kept before us, and swore if we did not turn in to that pasture, they would blow our brains out, (they had placed themselves opposite to a pair of Barrs, and had taken the Barrs down) they forced us in, when we had got in, Mr Prescot said put on. He took to the left, I to the right, towards a Wood, at the bottom of the Pasture intending, when I gained that, to jump my Horse & run afoot; just as I reached it, out started six officers, siesed my bridle, put their pistols to my Breast, ordered me to dismount, which I did.

One of them, who appeared to have the command there, and much of a Gentleman, asked me where I came from; I told him, he asked what time I left it; I told him, he seemed surprised, said Sr, may I crave your name. I answered my name is Revere, what said he, Paul Revere; I answered yes; the others abused me much; but he told me not to be afraid, no one should hurt me. I told him they would miss their Aim. He said they should not, they were only wait for some Deserters they expected down the Road. I told him I knew better, I knew what they were after; that I had alarmed the country all the way up, that their Boats were catch'd aground, and I should have 500 men there soon; one of them said they had 1500 coming; he seemed surprised and road off into the road, and informed them who took me, they came down immeditly on a full gallop, one of them (whom I since learned, was Major Mitchel of the 5th Regt) clapd his Pistol to my head, and said he was going to me some questions, if I did not tell the truth, he would blow my brains out. I told him I esteemed myself a man of truth, then he had stopped me on the highway, & made me a prisoner, I knew not by what right; I would tell him the truth; I was not afraid. He then asked me the same questions that they other did, and many more, but was more particular; I gave him much the same answers; he then ordered me to mount my horse, they first searched me for pistols. When I was mounted, the Major took the reins out of my hand, and said, by G-d Sr, you are not to ride with reins I assure you; and gave them to an officer on my right to lead me. He then Ordered 4 men out of the Bushes, and to mount their horses; they were country men which they had stopped who were going home; then ordered us to march. He said to me "We are now going towards your friends, and if you attempt to run, or we are insulted, we will blow your Brains out." When we had got into the road they formed a circle and ordered the prisoners in the centre & to lead me in the front.

We rid towards Lexington, a quick pace; they very often insulted me calling me Rebel, &c &c. after we had got about a mile, I was given to the sergant to lead, he was Ordered to take out his pistol (he rode with a hanger) and if I run, to execute the Major's sentence; When we got within about half a Mile of the Meeting house, we heard a gun fired; the Major asked me what it was for, I told him to alarm the country; he Ordered the four prisoners to dismount, they did, then one of the officers dismounted and cutt the Bridles, and Saddels, off the Horses, & drove them away, and told the men they might go about their business; I asked the Major to dismiss me, he said he would carry me, let the consequence be what it will; He then ordered us to march, when we got within sight of the

Meeting House, we heard a Volley of guns fired, as I supposed at the tavern, as an Alarm; the Major ordered us to halt, he asked me how far it was to Cambridge, and many more questions, which I answered; he then asked the Sergant, if his horse was tired, he said yes; he Ordered him to take my horse; I dismounted, the Sarjant mounted my horse; they cutt the Bridle & saddle off the Sarjant's horse & rode off down the road. I then went to the house where I left Messrs. Adams & Hancock, and told them what had happined; their friends advised them to go out of the way: I went with them, about two miles a cross road; after resting myself, I sett off with another man to go back to the Tavern, to enquire the News; when we got there, we were told the troops were within two miles. We went into the Tavern to git a Trunk of papers belonging to Col. Hancock, before we left the House, I saw the Ministeral Troops from the Chamber window. We made haste & had to pass thro' our Militia, who were on a green behind the Meeting house, to the number as I supposed, about 50 or 60. I went thro' them, as I passed I heard the commanding officer speake to his men to this purpose. "Lett the troops pass by & don't molest them, without they begin first" I had to go a cross Road, but had not got half Gun shot off when the Ministeral Troops appeared in sight behinde the Meeting House; they made a short halt, when a gun was fired. I heard the report, turned my head, and saw the smoake in front of the Troops, they immediately gave a great shout, ran a few paces, then the whole fired. I could first distinguish Iregular fireing, which I suppose was the advance Guard, and then platoons. At the time I could not see our Militia, for they were covered from me, by a house at the bottom of the Street, and further saith not.

—Paul Revere, April 18, 1775, in his deposition for the Massachusetts Provincial Congress.

house in the North End, much will have changed in America. While many know the story of Revere's famous night out, few are as familiar with his home life. Some things have changed on the property over the years: For example, a garden featuring 18th-century plants including lemon balm, sage and mint is not in its original position; and research has shown that Revere had a cow house on the property for a single milk cow, not uncommon in urban living at the time. But the quaint courtyard on North Square—the only home site on the Freedom Trail—lends a feel of what things might have been like during the period in which Revere and his family lived here.

The house, built in 1680, is the oldest surviving structure in downtown Boston and 90 percent of the infrastructure is original. The gray wooden home was built on the site of the former parsonage of the Second Church of Boston (built 1670) and was occupied by the minister, Increase Mather, and his family, including son Cotton Mather, the religious leader known for his influence over the Salem Witch Trials. The Great Fire of 1676 destroyed the home and it was rebuilt four years later. Merchant Robert Howard occupied the home before Revere, and added a partial third story to the existing structure.

Revere purchased the house in 1770 for 213 pounds and owned the property until 1800. His first wife, Sarah, his mother, Deborah, and five children (he eventually fathered sixteen) moved into the home. The neighborhood was one Revere knew well—it was where he had spent his childhood and his shop was a mere block and a half away. After the family sold the home, it was used for various purposes, including a candy shop and cigar factory. It was set to be demolished in 1902 until Revere's great-grandson, John P. Reynolds, purchased the home. It opened for tours to the public in 1908.

The self-guided tour includes four rooms and begins on the first level which houses a small kitchen used in the late 18th-century and a dark living room featuring oak beams and a snippet of 18th-century wallpaper. Twelve steps lead to the second level's "Best Chamber." While the room is set up as a bedroom, it was typical for a middle class colonial family like the Revere's to have a multipurpose room used for entertaining that showcased their finest possessions. It's here Revere may have joined his wife and other married couples for cards after a long day of casting. A glass case in the room exhibits documents explaining a Paul Revere and Abraham Lincoln connection (through marriage and politics).

Off the Best Chamber is the bedchamber said to have been occupied by Revere's mother, Deborah, until her death at the age of 73 in 1771. A highlight in the room is a sampler made by Revere's great-granddaughter Maria Revere Curtis, dated 1/25/1819. The bedchamber also showcases a small collection of photos of the home and a reproduction of paper money engraved by Paul Revere. The bedchamber leads to the second-floor exit, where visitors descend into the courtyard.

Impossible to overlook, a 900-pound bell, cast in 1804 by Paul Revere & Sons and sold in 1805 to the East Parish Church, in Bridgewater, Massachusetts, is on display near the garden, as is a copper bolt made by Revere for the USS *Constitution.*

The Pierce/Hichborn House (c. 1711), an early brick structure and example of Georgina architecture, owned by Revere's cousin, is adjacent to the Revere home. A combination ticket will buy you entry into both homes on days when guided tours are taking place at the Pierce/Hichborn House. Call ahead for information.

Tour Stop 13: Old North Church

Old North Church, 193 Salem Street, Boston, MA, (617) 523-6676, www.oldnorth.org. Jan–Feb, Tues–Sun 10–4; Mar–May daily 9–5; June–Oct, daily 9–6; Nov–Dec, daily 10–5. Presentations (6–7 minutes) made throughout the day. Check at gift shop for tour times. Suggested donation $3, self-guided tour brochure $1. 1-hour guided tours $8 for adults, $6 for students, seniors, military, and children under 6 (tickets available at gift shop). NORTH END

Built in 1723, this now Episcopal Church is officially named Christ Church in the City of Boston and is the oldest standing church in the city. Designed by William Price, the structure is based on Christopher Wren's London church designs and is comprised of Medford bricks in the English bond pattern. The 191-foot steeple (rebuilt twice) makes this Boston's tallest church. The bells one hears were cast in England in 1744, hung in 1745, and are the oldest in North America. The weathervane was the work of Shem Drowne, the designer of Faneuil Hall's well-known grasshopper weathervane. A crypt beneath the church contains 37 tombs, including the remains of Captain Samuel Nicholson, the first commander of the USS *Constitution,* and Major John Pitcairn, commander of the British Marines at Bunker Hill.

Although the church's architectural features are enough to warrant a visit, most flock to this sunny space to get a feeling for what happened April 18, 1775, the night of Paul Revere's Midnight Ride,

immortalized over eighty years later in Henry Wadsworth Longfellow's famous poem, "Paul Revere's Ride."

He said to his friend, "If the British march
By land or sea from the town to-night,
Hang a lantern aloft in the belfry-arch
Of the North-Church-tower, as a signal-light,—
One if by land, and two if by sea; . . ."

After 10:00 p.m. on that fateful night, sexton and caretaker of the church Robert Newman, hung two lit lanterns from the church's steeple—the highest point in Boston—to let Paul Revere, and Patriots in Charlestown know that British troops were on their way to Lexington and Concord via water, as opposed to land. Under the orders of British General Thomas Gage (a parishioner at the Old North Church), the troops were to arrest Sons of Liberty members Samuel Adams and John Hancock and try them for treason in London, as well as seize ammunition. While it's been noted that Newman held the lit lanterns for only a few seconds, the British troops saw the lights and stormed the church. It's said Newman escaped by jumping through the window located in the right rear of the church, now named in his honor and adorned with two lit lanterns given to the church by Gerald Ford. The night is acknowledged annually in mid-April with a lighting of the lanterns ceremony. The only remaining original lantern is on display in the Concord Museum.

The church was originally an Anglican Church and was created by contributions solicited from worshippers at the King's Chapel. King's Chapel was overcrowded and a need for another place

Opposite page: The steeple of Old North Church was made famous the night of Paul Revere's Midnight Ride.

of worship arose. Many of the Old North Church's parishioners, wealthy colonials, were loyal to the King. The luxurious style of the church, in sharp contrast to the simplicity of the Puritan churches is still evident today. The striking three-tiered English-made brass chandeliers were presented to the church in 1724 by worshipper Captain William Maxwell. The box pews were paid for by worshippers who showed their social status through the furnishings and wallpaper they used to decorate them. One can get an idea of a decorated pew from the Bay Pew, a gift from shipping merchants from the Bay of Honduras who assisted in financing the church's steeple. The organ on the balcony level was built in 1759 and was the first organ made in the Colonies. The oldest functioning clock in a public building in the U.S. is located here. The Avery & Bennett clock was donated by two church members who built the clock for the church in 1726. Gruchy's Angels, the four wooden winged figures around the organ are said to be stolen goods. Donated by Thomas Gruchy, who some say was a pirate, the Belgian-made angels were seized by Gruchy from a ship on its way to Quebec.

Today, the church is an active site and famous visitors from its past have included Franklin D. Roosevelt, who spoke here in 1920, and in 1975 Gerald Ford, who gave a replica of the famous lanterns to the church to honor the events of April 18, 1775. Queen Elizabeth II included the church on her American Bicentennial tour in 1976.

The church's gift shop next door has its own history. It was built in 1918 as the Waldensian

The Paul Revere statue on the Mall attracts throngs of visitors.

Reform Church for Protestant Italian immigrants who didn't speak English. Today the space is amply stocked with books pertaining to the American Revolution, as well as unique Boston-themed gifts and refrigerated bottled water. A small path between the Old North Church and the gift shop leads to the lovely St. Francis of Assisi Garden, tucked on the right.

Tour Stop 14: Copp's Hill Burying Ground

Copp's Hill Burying Ground, Hull Street, between Salem and Snow Hill streets (main entrance), Boston, MA, (617) 357-8300, www.cityofboston.gov/freedomtrail/coppshill.asp. Daily 9–5. Free. NORTH END

A tourist in Boston recently said, "If you've seen one cemetery, you've seen them all." Not the case in this historical city. Established in 1659, Copp's is the second-oldest burial ground in Boston and

Copp's Hill Burying Ground is situated at the highest point in the North End.

comes with its own unique history. Situated at the highest point in the North End, just a block from Old North Church, this burying ground was named after William Copp, an early settler and shoemaker who owned the land and lived on the southeast corner of the hill. Prior to becoming a burial ground, Copp's was the home of a windmill used for grinding corn and was called Windmill Hill.

The geography of Copp's has changed throughout the years and today, while it is still a great vantage point for Charlestown, it was once much more dramatic.

During the Revolution, this was an encampment for British troops. On June 17, 1775, the day of the Battle of Bunker Hill shots were fired from here to Charlestown and it is from this spot Major General Henry Clinton and Major General John Burgoyne of the British Army watched events unfold.

Today, a popular spot in Copp's is the grave of Boston Merchant Captain Daniel Malcolm. It's said the marks on his headstone are remains from bullets from British soldiers using his grave for target practice. Some say it was to spite his epitaph that included "a true son to the Liberty" and "an enemy to the opposition."

Ten thousand people are buried here and though it is now presented as one cemetery, the land was made up four different tracts. A section of Copp's was used for African-American burials and includes the remains of 1,000 freed slaves who are buried here in unmarked graves. Prince Hall, the founder of the first lodge of Black Freemasonry, is buried here, as is Edmund Hartt, builder of the USS *Constitution*; Cotton, Samuel, and Increase Mather; and Robert Newman.

"The hill at the north, rising to the height of about fifty feet above the sea, presented then on its north-west brow an abrupt declivity, long after known as Copp's Hill steeps. Its summit, almost level, extended between Prince and Charter streets towards Christ Church; thence south a gentle slope led to the water, which washed the south side of Prince and Charter streets towards Christ Church; thence south a gentle slope led to the water, which washed the south side of Prince street below, and the north side above Thacher street as far as Salem; eastward from the church, a gradual descent led to the North Battery, which was considered the bottom of the hill. Southeasterly the slope was still more gradual and terminated at the foot of north Square, leaving a knoll on the right, where at present stands the meeting-house of the Second Church."

—Copp's Hill as described by Dr. Snow in 1630, from *The History of Boston*

Tour Stop 15: USS *Constitution* ("Old Ironsides")

USS *Constitution,* 1 Constitution Road, Charlestown, MA, (617) 242-5670, www.history.navy.mil/ussconstitution/index.html. Nov.–Mar, Thurs–Sun 10–3:50; guided tours every half hour 10:30–3:30. Apr–Oct, Tues–Sun 10–5:50; guided tours every half hour 10:30–4:30. Free. CHARLESTOWN

This magnificent piece of marine history, docked in the Charlestown Navy Yard, is the oldest commissioned warship afloat in the world. Named after the U.S. Constitution, it is better known as "Old Ironsides," a nickname given to the ship during the War of 1812, when it was reported that cannonballs shot from the enemy British ship, the HMS *Guerrière,* appeared to bounce off the *Constitution*'s three-layer oak hull.

Designed by Joshua Humphreys, and built in 1794–1797, the ship was one of six frigates George Washington authorized to be built to help protect the American merchant fleet from attacks from Barbary pirates and the British. Built in Boston at the Edmund Hartt's shipyard, at a final cost of $302,700, the ship was constructed from 2,000 live oak trees and included castings, spikes, and bolts produced by the Paul Revere Foundry, as well as copper plates for the hull, imported from England by Paul Revere. The sails were sewn at the Granary Building in Boston.

First launched October 21, 1797, with a first sea sail on July 22, 1798, the ship had 33 entanglements, winning all. The undefeated ship battled during three wars: the Quasi War with France, the Barbary War, and the War of 1812.

The U.S.S. *Constitution* is the oldest commissioned warship afloat.

In 1830, the ship was declared unfit for sea. Due to a public outpouring of support following a poem written by then-twenty-one-year-old Oliver Wendell Holmes, the idea to scrap was scrapped, and plans for restoration began. Legend has it that Holmes read an article about the Navy's plans to scrap the ship in the *Boston Advertiser* and penned the famous poem, which appeared in the paper on September 15, 1830.

Old Ironsides

Oliver Wendell Holmes (written 1830)

Ay, tear her tattered ensign down!
Long has it waved on high,
And many an eye has danced to see
That banner in the sky;
Beneath it rung the battle shout,
And burst the cannon's roar; —
The meteor of the ocean air
Shall sweep the clouds no more.
Her deck, once red with heroes' blood,
Where knelt the vanquished foe,
When winds were hurrying o'er the flood,
And waves were white below,
No more shall feel the victor's tread,
Or know the conquered knee; —
The harpies of the shore shall pluck
The eagle of the sea!
Oh, better that her shattered hulk
Should sink beneath the wave;
Her thunders shook the mighty deep,
And there should be her grave;
Nail to the mast her holy flag,
Set every threadbare sail,
And give her to the god of storms,
The lightning and the gale!

Plans to scrap the ship were again made in 1905 but a public school campaign—started with children's pennies—led to the 1925 restoration.

The ship is still owned and operated by the U.S. Navy, and free tours (lasting about 45 minutes) are given by enthusiastic active Navy officers. After passing through security, expect a long line during peak times, though it's well worth the wait. In a

The U.S.S. *Constitution* is also known as "Old Ironsides." Wood engraving created 1872.

small area with benches, an introduction to the ship is provided before proceeding up the walkway and entering the second level, the gun deck. The ship—now comprised of 10 to 15 percent original materials—was built to carry forty-four guns (called cannons on land). Each gun, with carriage, weighs 6,5000 pounds and required nine to twelve men for handling. The guns recoil at 35–40 miles per hour.

It's on the gun deck that one cook prepared meals for up to 450 men (in 1812), consisting of heavily salted beef or pork that was steeped in a tub to rid the meat of some of the salt flavor. A nearby scuttlebutt, the original water cooler, is also housed here; soldiers were provided one gallon of water per day and could either drink the water or wash themselves or their clothes with the ration. Grog comprised of rum or whiskey was also served on this deck. The captain's cabin is currently closed to tours due to restoration to be completed in April 2011 (visitors will also note a temporary black-plastic roof as the top deck is being replaced).

Visitors to the U.S.S. *Constitution* Museum learn the history behind "Old Ironsides."

Visitors are led to narrow ladders comprised of rope that decent to the berth deck. Be forewarned: The space is claustrophobic and taller visitors won't be able to stand upright. It's here meals were consumed and sailors slept in close quarters on basic hammocks. Due to a lack of room, one half of the men would sleep while the others would work.

The bow of the berth deck was designated for ill and recovering soldiers while on the same level, but on the opposite side of the ship, was a well-constructed, partitioned area for the twenty to thirty officers who slept there in 1812. An additional level below the berth deck is not open to visitors.

Today, the ship leaves the dock six to eight times per year including an annual Turnaround Cruise on July 4. The ship uses no electrical power and runs on wind power provide by three masts. The main mast is 220 feet tall and it takes eighty to one hundred sailors to raise it.

Tour Stop 16: Bunker Hill Monument

Bunker Hill, Monument Square, Charlestown, MA, (617) 242-5641, www.nps.gov/bost/history culture/bhm.htm. Monument daily 9–4:30 (weather permitting). Monument Lodge daily 9–5. Free. CHARLESTOWN

A ten-minute leisurely walk from the USS *Constitution,* the Bunker Hill Monument has a deceptively peaceful vibe considering the bloody battle behind its history. Locals walk their dogs on the green surrounding the impressive 221-foot granite obelisk, and on good weather days, sun shines

The 221-foot Bunker Hill Monument dominates the skyline.

The Battle of Bunker Hill led to both American and British troop casualties.

down on the benches occupied by chatting tourists and those taking a respite in their picturesque neighborhood.

Technically, the famous battle of June 17, 1775, was on Breed's Hill (where the monument stands today) and not Bunker Hill, located north of Breed's. It's been noted the name of the battle is taken from the original plan to fight at Bunker Hill. The bloody battle counts causalities of 400–600 U.S. men and over 1,000 British. It's in this battle Dr. Joseph Warren was killed. It's said the British "won" the battle, yet the loss of lives was no victory for either side and the event made it apparent that both sides would not easily give up.

Word of the British plan to occupy the hills outside of Boston reached the U.S. Army, and General William Prescott led 1,200 colonial troops to the hill. Overnight, the men formed an encampment, to the surprise of the British, who then launched an attack the next afternoon and set Charlestown on fire. While some contend its legend, the famous command, "Don't fire 'til you see the whites of their eyes," may have been ordered by Prescott, and a plaque on the site honors the well-known

The famous words said to have been ordered by General William Prescott during the Battle of Bunker Hill, June 17, 1775.

The day,—perhaps the decisive day,—is come, on which the fate of America depends. My bursting heart must find vent at my pen. I have just heard, that our dear friend, Dr. Warren, is no more, but fell gloriously fighting for his country; saying, better to die honorably in the field, than ingloriously hang upon the gallows. Great is our loss. He has distinguished himself in every engagement, by his courage and fortitude, animating soldiers, and leading them on by his own example. A particular account of these dreadful, but I hope glorious days will be transmitted you, no doubt, in the exactest manner. "The race is not to the swift, nor the battle to the strong; but the God of Israel is he, that giveth strength and power unto his people. Trust in him at all times, ye people, pour out your hearts before him: God is a refuge for us." Charleston is laid in ashes. The battle began upon our intrenchments upon Bunker's hill, Saturday morning about three o'clock, and has not ceased yet, and is now three o'clock Sabbath afternoon.
It is expected they will come out over the Neck to-night, and a dreadful battle must ensue. Almighty God, cover the heads of our countrymen, and be a shield to our dear friends! How many have fallen we know not. The constant roar of the cannon is so distressing that we can not eat, drink, or sleep. May we be supported and sustained in the dreadful conflict. I shall tarry here till it is thought unsafe by my friends, and then I have secured myself a retreat at your brother's who has kindly offered me part of his house. I cannot compose myself to write any further at present. I will add more as I hear further.
—Letter to John Adams in Philadelphia from wife Abigail Adams. Weymouth, Mass. Sunday June 18, 1775.

phrase. The first major battle of the American Revolution left many rattled and anxious about the future of Boston and their country.

Those wishing to climb the 294-step monument, erected in 1794 and built with granite from Quincy, should enter the small monument building run by the National Park Service, featuring portraits of Major General Henry Clinton of the British Army, Captain John Linzee of the British Royal Navy, and General John Stark of the New Hampshire Militia. The exit of the monument building leads to the "lobby" of the monument itself and features an 18-foot wooden version of the obelisk. This was the first monument erected on this site (1794) and was originally dedicated to William Prescott (on the

A statue of William Prescott is proudly displayed before the Bunker Hill Monument.

Massachusetts Gate side of the grounds, a large statue of William Prescott, is proudly displayed). In 1823 plans to commemorate all lives lost at the site were developed and a bake sale in 1840 helped to raise the much-needed funds for the monument that stands here today.

Those wishing to climb the stairs are met with the reward of a good lookout point but should keep in mind that children under 14 must be accompanied by an adult and there is no elevator. Those with health issues or suffering from claustrophobia will want to admire the monument from outside.

PLACES TO VISIT NEARBY

Battle of Bunker Hill Museum, 43 Monument Square, www.nps.gov/bost/historyculture/bhmuseum.htm. Daily 9–5. Free. The museum, completed in 2007, isn't extensive but historical photos of Bunker/Breed's Hill, exhibits about Charlestown and the monument, as well as memorabilia including postage stamps and decorative plates commemorating the Battle of Bunker Hill make it worth the stop. A gift shop with tote bags, reproduction of historic documents such as a call to arms under General Washington and a 1775 British Army recruiting poster can be found here. Disposable cameras and National Park handbooks are also for sale. CHARLESTOWN

Boston Athenaeum, 10½ Beacon Street, (617) 227-0270, www.bostonathenaeum.org. Mon 8:30–8, Tues–Fri 8:30–5:30, Sat 9–4; closed Sat May 23–Aug 29. Introductory tours Wed at noon (meet at the circulation desk); art and architecture tours Tues and Thurs at 3; reservations required (617-227-0270 ext. 279). Free. Founded in 1807, this is the oldest continuously circulating library in the U.S. The library—which overlooks the Granary Burying Ground—now occupies the Edward Clarke Cabot–designed National Historic Landmark, constructed 1847–1849. Although this is a working library—featuring resources on Boston history—much of the space is used as an art gallery and regular events including teas, book clubs, and concerts take place in the pristine and elegant space. BEACON HILL

The John F. Kennedy Library and Museum is one of twelve presidential libraries.

John F. Kennedy Library and Museum, Columbia Park, Congress Street, (617) 514-1600, www.jfk library.org. Daily 9–5. Adults $12, seniors (62+) $10; students $10; ages 13–17 $9; children 12 and under free. Set on a 10-acre park, this site is dedicated to our thirty-fifth president, and is one of the twelve presidential libraries administered by the National Archives and Records Administration. While scholars make use of historical documents and resources here, the facilities are open to the public. A visitor's ticket includes an introductory film (3:55 p.m. is the last showing of the day) as well as access to exhibits including a re-creation of the July 13, 1960, Democratic Convention in Los Angeles, and a full-size mockup of the 1960 Kennedy-Nixon debate, the first televised presidential debate in U.S. history. SOUTH BOSTON

Museum of African American History/Black Heritage Trail, 46 Joy Street, (617) 720-2991, www.afroammuseum.org. Museum Mon–Sat 10–4 (hours are subject to change, call (617) 742-5415 for more information). Guided Black Heritage Trail tours Memorial Day–Labor Day, Mon-Sat at 10 and 2 and year-round Mon-Sat at 2. Free. The museum, which is "dedicated to preserving, conserving, and accurately interpreting the contributions of African-Americans in New England from the colonial period through the 19th century," features rotating exhibits and provides maps for self-guided tours of the Black Heritage Trail (1.6 miles and comprised of the following sites: Robert Gould Shaw and 54th Regiment Memorial; George Middleton

House, the Phillips School; John J. Smith House, Charles Street Meeting House, Lewis and Harriet Hayden House, John Coburn House, Smith Court Residences, Abiel Smith School, and the African American Meeting House). BEACON HILL

The New England Holocaust Memorial, Carmen Park, Congress Street, (617) 457-8755, www.nehm.com. Always open. Free. Located on the Freedom Trail, this memorial, created in 1995, is dedicated to six million Jews killed in the Holocaust. Six glass towers—internally lit and emitting smoke—are a metaphor for the six million people and six main death camps, and are symbolic of menorah candles. Each of the poignant 54-foot towers is etched with a million numbers to represent those who died, and suggests the arm tattoos of the victims. The towers also include quotes from Holocaust survivors. GOVERNMENT CENTER

Glass towers emit steam at the New England Holocaust Memorial.

Otis House Museum, 141 Cambridge Street (enter on Lynde Street), (617) 227-3957 ext. 256, www.historicnewengland.org. Daily 11–4:30. $8. This stately Federal-style house built in 1796—one of three Charles Bulfinch designed for his friend Harrison Gray Otis (1765–1848)—offers tours on the hour and half hour and is a good depiction of how the governing class lived. Otis served in the Massachusetts House of Representatives (1796–1797 and 1802–1805), U.S. House of Representatives (1797–1801), was a member of the U.S. Senate (1817–1822), and mayor of Boston (1829–1832). He was known for strongly opposing the War of 1812. This is also the site of the Historic New England headquarters; a library, museum, and gift shop are on the premises. BEACON HILL

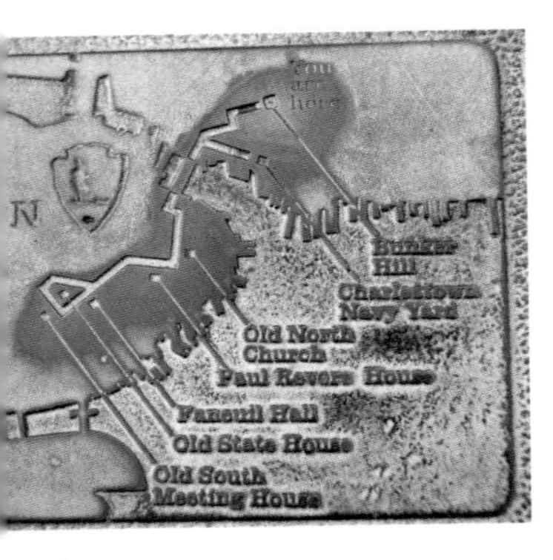

Paul Revere Mall, Hanover Street (front entrance). Always open. Free. Tucked behind the Old North Church and in the front of St. Stephen's, this is the site of the bronze statue of Paul Revere on his horse, by Cyrus Edwin Dallin. Once a pasture, the now buzzing outdoor space—also known as "the Prado"—features the occasional street musician, running fountain, and a welcome respite from sightseeing. The walls of the outdoor mall are covered with plaques chockfull of North End history. NORTH END

Quincy Market, 1375 Washington Street, (617) 742-7275, Mon–Sat 10–9, Sun noon–6; www.faneuilhallmarketplace.com. Outdoor restaurants and pubs have their own hours. Free. Located directly behind Faneuil Hall (the small space in between the two buildings is home to scheduled street performers; see Web site for calendar), and part of the Faneuil Hall Marketplace, the building was constructed 1824–1826 to provide space for additional shops and for outdoor carts. Named after Mayor Josiah Quincy, this two-story, 27,000-square-foot space, designed by Alexander Parris, showcases an exterior of New England granite and features Doric columns. The marketplace was originally on the harbor's edge before the use of landfill, and the addition of city streets changed the landscape. Today, this frenetic market features fast food from around the globe, including Thai, Greek, and Italian cuisine, a far cry from when the market sold almost all produce and dairy products. The outdoor section of the building is full of visitors and souvenir pushcarts. GOVERNMENT CENTER

St. Stephen's Church (former New North Church), 401 Hanover Street, (617) 523-1230. Generally Mon–Fri 7:30–4, Sat 3:30–5:30, Sun 10–12:30; call to verify hours. Free. Just across the street from the Paul Revere Mall, with a magnificent white bell tower, this is the only remaining standing Charles Bulfinch church. Built in 1804 as the New North Congregational Church, it became the Second Unitarian church in 1814. In 1862, it became known as St. Stephen's. Rose Kennedy was baptized in the beautiful and austere space on July 23, 1890. The lobby includes historic photos of the church. NORTH END

USS *Constitution* Museum, Charlestown Navy Yard, Building 22, (617) 426-1812, www.ussconstitutionmuseum.org. Apr 1–Oct 31, daily 9–6; Nov 1–Mar 31, daily 10–5, closed Thanksgiving, Christmas Day, and New Year's Day. Admission by donation. A minute's walk from the ship, this interactive family-friendly museum provides additional historical information, ship memorabilia, and educational exhibits about the famous vessel. Highlights include the impressive circa-1962 model of the ship and a 200-year timeline. The museum has a gift shop stocked with cold drinks, post cards, sweatshirts, and souvenirs including a USS *Constitution* ship in a bottle kit. Free maps of the area are also available. CHARLESTOWN

WHERE TO STAY

The good news is, Boston is chockfull of hotels. The bad news is, accommodations are often pricey. Check rates in advance and keep in mind rooms fill up during Pride Week (June), Boston Harborfest (July), and the December holidays. Deals for some hotels can often be found on Priceline (www.price line.com) and Orbitz (www.orbitz.com).

Holiday Inn Boston at Beacon Hill, 5 Blossom Street, (617) 742-7630, www.hisboston.com. A ten- to fifteen-minute walk to the Massachusetts State House and Boston Common, and just a couple of minutes' walk to the Otis House, this budget-friendly high-rise accommodates visitors without a hefty price tag. The 303 rooms include free Wi-Fi and cable television, and suites with refrigerators are available. The location—a safe and busy area near Mass General Hospital—is bustling with coffee shops and inexpensive dining options, perfect for gearing up for a day on the Freedom Trail. BEACON HILL

The Langham, 250 Franklin Street, (617) 451-1900, www.boston.langhamhotels.com. This 318-room hotel is nestled in the Financial District, close to Fanueil Hall. Once the Federal Reserve Bank of Boston, the hotel showcases two Andrew Wyeth murals on the second floor and historic photographs of the building in its former incarnation on the fifth floor. Tasteful, traditional rooms include Italian-marble bathrooms. A 2008-renovated fitness center and spa featuring Chinese medicine and treatments make it easy to relax or burn off steam after sightseeing. Bond restaurant (see below) is housed here. FINANCIAL DISTRICT

The Liberty Hotel, 215 Charles Street, (617) 224-4000, www.libertyhotel.com. Originally built as the Charles Street Jail in 1851, this National Historical Landmark is a repurposed architectural gem that's been abuzz since it opened in 2007 after a $150 million renovation. Original exposed brick and the former guard catwalks accent the stunning lobby of this luxury hotel. The majority of the 298 rooms are in a new tower and include flat-screen TVs, imported linens, and high-speed Wi-Fi, and are decorated in soothing tones. A 24-hour fitness center, and on-site restaurants and bars (see Clink, below) are the perfect way to unwind after a long day on the Freedom Trail. BEACON HILL

The chic Liberty Hotel was once home to the Charles Street Jail.

Nine Zero, 90 Tremont Street, (617) 772-5800, www.ninezero.com. Directly across the street from the Granary Burying Ground, this swank, design-oriented hotel wows with its bold color scheme and hip vibe. Abstract art adorns moderately sized rooms outfitted with everything needed for a comfortable stay, including a featherbed and pillow menu. A complimentary wine reception (5–6 p.m.) is included with overnight stay and a helpful staff keeps this bustling spot, part of the Kimpton hotel chain, running smoothly. Pet packages are available. DOWNTOWN

The Nine Zero sign lets visitors know they've arrived at this swank Kimpton hotel.

Omni Parker House, 60 School Street, (617) 227-8600, www.omninotels.com. Located on the Freedom Trail (King's Chapel is just across the street from the School Street entrance, and the Granary Burying Ground is seconds from the Tremont Street entrance), this historic "giant B and B" underwent a multimillion-dollar extensive renovation that was completed in 2008. Founded in 1855, this is the longest continuously operated hotel in the U.S and boasts a former guest list including Charles Dickens, Ralph Waldo Emerson, Sarah Bernhardt, Joan Crawford, and James Dean. The 551 rooms have retained their historic charm yet have modern amenities like luxurious bedding and Wi-Fi. The hotel offers family packages and is pet friendly. An elegant lobby features all-American carved oak and original bronze elevator doors leading to the famed Parker Restaurant (see below). The Press Room on the lower level is where John F. Kennedy declared his candidacy for U.S. Congress. DOWNTOWN

Residence Inn Boston Harbor on Tudor Wharf, 34-44 Charles River Avenue, (617) 242-9000, www.marriott.com. If you plan to spend a good deal of time at the USS *Constitution* and Bunker Hill, this eight-floor, 168-room Marriott hotel is convenient, located across the bridge from the North End in Charlestown, just minutes from both sites and within an easy walking distance. Rooms with kitchens are available, as are allergy-friendly accommodations. Guests receive a complimentary hot breakfast. Pets are allowed with deposit. CHARLESTOWN

WHERE TO EAT

Boloco, 27 School Street, (617) 778-6750, www.boloco.com. This certified Green Restaurant is part of a local chain specializing in "inspired burritos." Pick a style (such as Cajun, teriyaki, or Caesar), add a protein (choices include baked organic tofu, braised pork *carnitas,* and grilled all-white chicken) and request a size (regular or mini) for a hearty, healthy inexpensive meal that can be rounded out with a salad or smoothie. A casual space and free Wi-Fi, this is on the same block as King's Chapel, the First Public School site, and the Old Corner Bookstore. DOWNTOWN

Bond, 250 Franklin Street, (617) 956-8765, www.bondboston.com. History buffs will recognize this address as the former Federal Reserve Bank of Boston. Twenty-foot ceilings, the original seal of the bank, and a mirrored bar sets the scene for this glamorous restaurant in the Langham Hotel that opened in January 2009. Chef Mark Sapienza's menu spans the globe and includes must-have New England standbys like a creamy and perfectly seasoned New England clam chowder, and lobster roll made with house mayo and set atop a buttery toasted roll. The crispy potato chips are a not-to-be-missed specialty of the house. No breakfast. FINANCIAL DISTRICT

Café Vittoria, 290-296 Hanover Street, (617) 227-7606, www.vittoriacaffe.com. A short jaunt from the Old North Church, this old-world café, established in 1929, features tin ceilings and open window front and is a great spot for a respite and people-watching. Expert baristas are in full view as they steam milk for some of the best cappuccinos in the city. Italian sweets like the *cannolis*, *tiramisu* and *spumoni* make for a perfect late-afternoon sugar boost after a long day on the Freedom Trail. Cash only. NORTH END

Clink, 215 Charles Street, (617) 224-4004, www.clinkrestaurant.com. Located on the lobby level of the Liberty Hotel, this swank spot attracts a hip crowd that isn't taken aback by sitting in a space that retains walls from the jail cells that once housed prisoners here. Today the lively restaurant with exposed brick is surprisingly warm and inviting despite its history. Chef Joseph Margate offers modern-American seasonal dishes like chilled tomato soup that bursts with farm-fresh flavor and is accented with pillows of smoked yogurt, buttery halibut served in a fragrant herb foam with firm green chickpeas, and perfectly seared sea scallops alongside porcini mushrooms, parsnips, and dates. Desserts like the not-too-sweet Valrhona chocolate tart are worth the caloric splurge. The Massachusetts State House is the closest Freedom Trail site to this location. BEACON HILL

Todd English's Figs Restaurant wows with its gourmet pizzas.

Figs, 42 Charles Street, (617) 742-3447 and 67 Main Street, Charlestown, MA, (617) 242-2229, www.toddenglish.com. Part of Boston chef Todd English's restaurant empire, Figs is a sophisticated yet moderately priced dining option featuring gourmet thin-crust pizzas like the must-order spicy gulf shrimp with leeks. Italian-inspired salads and pastas round out the menu. The Charlestown location is minutes from the Bunker Hill monument and the Beacon Hill restaurant is a great lunch spot before a day on the Common. BEACON HILL AND CHARLESTOWN

Parker's Restaurant, 60 School Street, (617) 227-8600, www.omnihotels.com. If only the beautiful dark oak walls of this historic restaurant could talk: JFK proposed to Jacqueline Onassis at table #40 and Malcolm X (a busboy in the early 1940s) and Ho Chi Minh (a baker from 1912 to 1913) can be counted as former employees. The history of this dark and sophisticated fine-dining spot includes culinary markers as well: It's here the Boston cream pie (now Massachusetts' official state dessert) and the Parker roll (a dinner roll made with milk) were invented. A menu including classics like chilled shrimp cocktail, French onion soup, and a 14-ounce New York sirloin are sure to please (and come with a hefty price tag). Located in the historic Omni Parker House hotel, the restaurant is a minute to School Street sites and the Boston Common. It makes for an elegant evening after a day of touring. No lunch Saturday and Sunday. No dinner Sunday. DOWNTOWN

Regina Pizza, 11½ Thatcher Street, (617) 227-0765, www.reginapizzeria.com. One bite of the piping-hot, secret-recipe Neapolitan crust with tangy tomato sauce and fresh toppings and you'll understand why this is award-winning pizza. Established in 1926, this three-generation family business often has a crowd out front who know it's worth the wait to enter the modest space—adorned with photos of famous folk who have dined here, from Teddy Kennedy to Rob Lowe—and order from the simple menu (only pizza!). It's a great lunch spot after a tour of the Paul Revere House. No breakfast. NORTH END

Famous former patrons of the Union Oyster House include Daniel Webster and John F. Kennedy.

Union Oyster House, 41 Union Street, (617) 227-2750, www.unionoysterhouse.com. Boston's oldest restaurant (1826), this designated historic landmark is directly on the Freedom Trail (close to Faneuil Hall) and across from the Holocaust Memorial. Daniel Webster was known for dining at the oyster bar, and years later, J.F.K. made this a regular haunt (his favorite booth is designated with a plaque on the second level). The menu is loaded with sandwiches, salads, and soups—including, of course, a satisfying traditional New England clam chowder. No breakfast. GOVERNMENT CENTER

Warren Tavern, 2 Pleasant Street, (617) 241-8142, www.warrentavern.com. Named for Dr. Joseph Warren, this is a casual joint about a five-minute walk from the Bunker Hill Monument. It's the oldest tavern in the state (the building dates back to 1780) and Paul Revere and George Washington spent time here back in the day. Today you'll find a mix of locals hanging at the bar and cozy tables, grabbing a beer and enjoying a half-pound Angus burger or hearty choices like the Thanksgiving sandwich (turkey, stuffing, and cranberry on the bread of your choice) served with a heap of crispy, salty fries. No breakfast. CHARLESTOWN

Glossary

Boston Tea Party: Colonists dumped tea into Boston Harbor on December 16, 1773, in response to the Tea Act.

Colonies: Considered British America, the 13 original colonies included Connecticut, Delaware, Georgia, Maryland, Massachusetts, New Hampshire, New Jersey, New York, North Carolina, South Carolina, Pennsylvania, Rhode Island, and Virginia. They opposed British rule, leading to the American Revolution.

congregation: An organized religious group, often belonging to a specific church/place of worship.

Epitaph: A message inscribed on a gravestone or tomb.

Federalist style: A style of architecture (1780–1815) inspired by Greek, Roman, and English architecture. Often includes archways and decorative moldings/details.

Georgian style: A style of architecture (1720–1840) known for its symmetry; named after King George III.

Puritans: Protestants opposed to the Church of England.

regiment: A military unit consisting of two or more groups/battalions.

sentry: A solider who stands guard/keeps watch.

Sons of Liberty: A clandestine group of organized Patriots who worked in opposition to British rule. Included Paul Revere, John Adams, and John Hancock.

Stamp Act (1765): A British tax on the American Colonies on items including printed materials required a stamp to show taxes had been paid. The tax enraged the Patriots because it was designed to fund the British troops in the Colonies and pay British war debt.

Sugar Tax (1764): A British tax on the American Colonies on sugar imported from the West Indies.

Tea Act (1773): Gave the British East India Company a monopoly on tea exported to the British Colonies.

Writs of Assistance: Search warrants that allowed any search and seizure of a ship or building without explanation.

Additional Reading

Adams, John. *Diary and Autobiography of John Adams.* L. H. Butterfield, editor. Cambridge, MA: The Belknap Press of Harvard University Press, 1961.

Allison, Robert J. *A Short History of Boston.* Beverly: Commonwealth Editions, 2004.

Andrews, Joseph L., Jr. *Revolutionary Boston, Lexington, and Concord: The Shots Heard 'Round the World!* Beverly: Commonwealth Editions, 2002.

Forbes, Esther. *Paul Revere and the World He Lived In.* New York: Mariner Books, 1999.

Goldfeld, Alex R. *The North End: A Brief History of Boston's Oldest Neighborhood.* Charleston/Salem: The History Press, 2009.

Gross, Robert A. *The Minutemen and their World*. New York: Hill & Wang, 2001.

Hallahan, William H. *The Day the American Revolution Began: 19 April 1775.* New York: Harper Perennial, 2001.

Jones, Howard Mumford, and Bessie Zaban Jones. *The Many Voices of Boston: A Historical Anthology 1630–1975*. Boston: Little, Brown & Company, 1975.

Lancaster, Bruce. *The American Revolution.* New York: Mariner Books, 2001.

Martin, Tyrone, G. *A Most Fortunate Ship: A Narrative History of Old Ironsides*. Annapolis: U.S. Naval Institute Press, 2003.

O'Connor, Thomas H. *Boston A to Z.* Cambridge: Harvard University Press, 2000.

Raphael, Ray. *A People's History of the American Revolution: How Common People Shaped the Fight for Independence.* New York: Harper Perennial, 2002.

Young, Alfred F. *Liberty Tree: Ordinary People and the American Revolution.* New York: NYU Press, 2006.

Index

Adams, Abigail, 42, 71
Adams, John, 3, 8, 42, 43
Adams, Samuel, 8, 25, 31, 37, 48–49, 59

Battle of Bunker Hill, 4, 5, 13, 42, 70, 73
Battle of Bunker Hill Museum, 73
Beacon Hill, 6, 12–25, 35–39, 73–74, 75, 78, 79, 82
Black Heritage Trail, 6, 74–75
Blackstone, William, 1–2, 12
Boloco, 81
Bond restaurant, 7, 81
Boston African American National Historic Site, 16
Boston Athenaeum, 73–74
Boston Common, 1, 5, 12–16, 46
Boston Latin School, 30, 31
Boston Massacre, 3, 15, 37, 42, 44–46
Boston Massacre Memorial, 15
Boston National Historical Park, 5
Boston Public Latin School, 30–32
Boston Tea Party, 4
Bulfinch, Charles, 6, 8, 17, 27, 31, 49
Bulfinch State House, 43
Bunker Hill, 4, 5, 69–72
Bunker Hill Monument, 69–72

Café Vittoria, 81–82
Central Burying Ground, 15
Charles Street Jail, 7, 79
Charlestown, 64–72, 73, 77, 80, 82, 84
Chilton, Mary, 28
Clink restaurant, 82
Common. *See* Boston Common
Copp's Hill Burying Ground, 5, 62–63
Cotton, John, 31
Crafts, Thomas, Jr., 41

Downtown area, 26–34, 40–46, 79, 80, 81, 83
Dyer, Mary, 12, 20

Emerson, Ralph Waldo, 6, 31, 38
Emerson, William, 28

Faneuil Hall, 5, 47–50
Faneuil, Peter, 9, 25, 47
Figs restaurant, 82
Financial District, 78, 81
First Public School, 5, 29–32
Franklin, Benjamin, 5, 9, 29, 31
Freedom Trail Information Center, 14
Freeman, James, 27
Frog Pond, 12, 14–15

Garrison, William Lloyd, 22
Government Center, 6, 47–50, 75, 76, 84
Granary Burying Ground, 5, 22, 24–25, 44

Hancock, John, 3, 9, 25, 31, 59
Hartt, Edmund, 63, 64
Hawthorne, Nathaniel, 6
Holiday Inn Boston at Beacon Hill, 78
Holmes, Oliver Wendell, 66
Hopper, William, 31
Hutchinson, Thomas, 31

Information Center, 14

John F. Kennedy Library and Museum, 6, 74

Kennedy, John F., 6–7, 20, 74
King's Chapel, 5, 26–28, 59–60
King's Chapel Burying Ground, 28

Lambert's Marketplace, 39
Langham, The, 7, 78
Liberty Hotel, The, 7, 79
Longfellow, Henry Wadsworth, 38, 59

Malcolm, Daniel, 63
Mass Meeting in Aid of
  Recruitment, 13
Massachusetts State House, 5,
  17–20
Mather, Cotton, 31, 55, 63
Mather, Samuel, 31, 63
Museum of African American
  History/Black Heritage Trail,
  74–75

National Parks Service, 7
New England Holocaust Memorial,
  6, 75
Newman, Robert, 9–10, 59, 63
Nicholson, Samuel, 57
Nine Zero, 79
Norman B. Leventhal Walk to the
  Sea, 6
North End, 51–63, 76, 77, 81–82, 83

Old Corner Bookstore, 5, 33–34
Old Ironsides. *See* USS *Constitution*
Old North Church, 5, 57–61
Old South Meeting House, 5, 35–39
Old State House Museum, 5, 40–43
Omni Parker House, 6, 80
Otis House Museum, 6, 75
Otis, James, Jr. 10, 25, 42, 48

Pain, Elizabeth, 28
Paine, Robert Treat, 31
Park Street Church, 5, 21–23
Parker's Restaurant, 83
Paul Revere Mall, 76
Paxton, Charles, 27
Pierce/Hichborn House, 56
Prescott, William, 10, 70–71, 72
Preston, Thomas, 44, 46

Quincy Market, 76

Regina Pizza, 83
Residence Inn Boston Harbor on
  Tudor Wharf, 80
Revere, Paul, 1, 2, 3, 4, 5, 10, 18, 25,
  27, 46, 51–56, 57, 58, 59, 64
Robert Gould Shaw Memorial, 16

Sacred Cod, 19, 20
Saturday Literary Club, 6
Schofield, William, 5
Shaw, Robert Gould, 11, 16
Shirley, William 27
Soldiers and Sailors Monument, 15
Sons of Liberty, 59
South Boston, 74
St. Stephen's Church, 77

Tea Tax, 4, 36–37
Townsend Act, 42, 44

Union Oyster House, 84
USS *Constitution* Museum, 77
USS *Constitution* ("Old Ironsides"),
  1, 5, 64–68, 77

Warren, Joseph, 11
Warren Tavern, 84
Washington, George, 20, 27, 64
Winthrop, John, 2, 11, 28
Winthrop, Robert Charles, 13–14